Brittany

◇

By Richard Beauchamp

Contents

Training Your Brittany 80

By Charlotte Schwartz
Be informed about the importance of training your Brittany from the basics of house-training and understanding the development of a young dog to executing obedience commands (sit, stay, down, etc.).

Health Care of Your Brittany 107

Discover how to select a qualified veterinarian and care for your dog at all stages of life. Topics include vaccination scheduling, skin problems, dealing with external and internal parasites and the medical and behavioral conditions common to the breed.

Your Senior Brittany 136

Recognize the signs of an aging dog, both behavioral and medical; implement a senior-care program with your veterinarian and become comfortable with making the final decisions and arrangements for your senior Brittany.

Showing Your Brittany 144

Experience the dog show world, including different types of shows and the making of a champion. Go beyond the conformation ring to field, obedience and agility trials.

KENNEL CLUB BOOKS: **BRITTANY**
ISBN: 1-59378-285-3

Copyright © 1999 • **Revised American Edition: Copyright © 2004**
Kennel Club Books, Inc., 308 Main Street, Allenhurst, NJ 07711 USA
Cover Design Patented: US 6,435,559 B2 • Printed in South Korea

Photographs by Carol Ann Johnson
with additional photos by Norvia Behling, Mary Bloom, T.J. Calhoun, Carolina Biological Supply, Doskocil, Isabelle Français, James Hayden-Yoav, James R. Hayden, RBP, Bill Jonas, Dwight R. Kuhn, Dr. Dennis Kunkel, Mikki Pet Products, Phototake, Jean Claude Revy, Alice Roche, Dr. Andrew Spielman, Karen Taylor and Alice van Kempen.

The publisher wishes to thank the following owners for allowing their dogs to be photographed for this book: Emile J Berlet, Thierry Bouty, William Crépelle, Moira Doherty, Barbara Dunkling, Steve Izod and Linda McCartney.

Illustrations by Patricia Peters

The Brittany was developed by combining the desirable traits of
spaniels and setters into a breed that could assist hunters in locating
game. The result was an exceptional breed of dog—a natural beauty
who is an all-round wonderful worker and companion.

BRITTANY

There are far more pure-bred breeds of dog existing throughout the world today than most people will have the opportunity to see in a lifetime. As strikingly dissimilar and diversified as these breeds are, they all trace back to one common ancestor—*Canis lupus*—the wolf. Everything dogs are and everything they do was passed down through thousands upon thousands of generations to what is universally considered "man's best friend."

Archeological discoveries lead us to believe that the relationship between man and dog or, as it was in the beginning, man and wolf, was based upon man's struggle to survive in the most inhospitable of times. The wolf's prowess as a hunter was something that early man could not help but observe and there seems to be evidence that man himself may have put some of those techniques to use as well. Then too, the wolf had many social habits similar to man's own and this undoubtedly assisted in creating that first step toward compatibility.

In *The Natural History of Dogs*, authors Richard and Alice Feinnes classify most dogs as having descended from one of four major groups: the Dingo Group, the Greyhound Group, the Nordic Group and the Mastiff Group. All four trace back to separate and distinct branches of the wolf family.

The Dingo Group traces its origin to the Asian wolf (*Canis lupus pallipes*). Two well-known examples of the Dingo Group are the Basenji and, through the admixture of several European breeds, the Rhodesian Ridgeback.

The Greyhound Group descends from a coursing-type

The Brittany is a celebrated sporting dog, gregarious and obedient.

A relative of the Brittany is the larger Breton Spaniel. This is Int. Ch. Fanchio de Cornonaille of Breton.

Eng. Ch. Aotrou de Cornonaille in a photo circa 1930. This dog resembles an English Springer Spaniel of setter type.

A dog resembling the Brittany of the early 1900s, who was a noted worker and prizewinner of his time.

relative of the Asian wolf. The group includes all those dogs that hunt by sight and are capable of great speed. The Greyhound itself, the Afghan Hound and the Saluki are all examples. They are not true hounds in that they do not hunt by scent.

The Arctic or Nordic Group of dogs is a direct descendant of the rugged Northern wolf (*Canis lupus*). Included in the many breeds of this group are the Alaskan Malamute, Chow Chow and German Shepherd Dog.

The fourth classification, the Mastiff Group, owes its primary heritage to the Tibetan wolf (*Canis lupus chanco* or *laniger*). This group encompasses the greatest diversity of breeds and the extreme diversity indicates the descendants are not entirely of pure blood. The specific breeds included have undoubtedly been influenced by descendants of the other three groups. This influence is of consequence in that some Mastiff Group breeds have acquired characteristics that others do not share at all.

Of importance here is the fact that the Mastiff Group is known to include many of the scenting breeds—breeds which find game by the use of their olfactory senses (their noses) rather than by sight. These breeds include those we now classify as gundogs or sporting dogs well as the true hounds.

As man became more sophisticated and his lifestyle more complex, he found he could produce dogs which could suit his specific needs from the descendants of the wolf. Often these needs were based upon the manner in which man himself went after game and the terrain in which he was forced to do so.

By this time man had taken control of the individual dogs that mated. Particular characteristics were prized and inbreeding practices employed to perpetuate these characteristics.

It is an established fact that dogs and horses traveled all over the world with their owners during the first Crusades. Even if the animals that left their native lands were of a pure strain, there can be little doubt that the offspring they produced along their journeys were the result of an infusion of foreign blood. English, Spanish, French and Arabian bloodlines were thus coursing through the veins of the animals that accompanied the Crusaders back to their homeland.

One type of hunting dog popularly used at that time retained the wolf characteristic of pursuing the prey until it was cornered or captured and killed. This practice is more or less typical of the dogs known today as the true hounds. While their tenacity in pursuit was held in high regard, the hound's willing-

GENUS *CANIS*
Dogs and wolves are members of the genus *Canis*. Wolves are known scientifically as *Canis lupus* while dogs are known as *Canis domesticus*. Dogs and wolves are known to interbreed. The term "canine" derives from the Latin derived word *Canis*. The term "dog" has no scientific basis but has been used for thousands of years. The origin of the word "dog" has never been authoritatively ascertained.

ness to chase could continue on and on for miles if need be, and some men found keeping up rather tiresome or impossible.

Thus was born a need for the hunting dog that did not follow through with the chase or the attack. Their job was not to do the hunting or killing, but rather to assist the human hunter by finding, flushing out or retrieving the game. These dogs worked quietly so as not to scare away the birds and, like any good assistant, they obeyed their masters' commands without hesitation.

During the Middle Ages, before guns were invented, hunters used nets and trained hawks to capture their prey. Assisting them were little dogs that some believe actually had originated in Spain. The Latin word for Spain is *Hispania* and it is from Hispania that the name "Spaniells" (later "spaniels") evolved.

Once the game was located, some of these Spaniells would drop to the ground, remaining motionless until the hunter arrived to throw his net over the birds. These "Setting Spaniells" were used in the development of the breeds that became known as our modern-day Irish, English and Gordon Setters.

Another group of the Spaniells was trained to find birds and drive them out of the under-brush so that they could be pursued and captured by falcons. These dogs were called "Springing Spaniells" because of their talent for springing or flush-ing birds from their hiding places. Since they most often had to track their prey through dense shrubs and tangled thickets, the dogs needed compact, smaller bodies and powerful legs to help them move through the difficult terrain that often stopped other dogs cold.

The dogs had long silky coats that offered protection against the thistles and brambles of the dense undergrowth. The tails of these dogs were docked to prevent them from being caught in the brush. They had higher rounded fore-heads, which were thought to

have shielded their eyes against branches. Their long lobular ears gathered and channeled scent molecules to their large ultra-sensitive noses.

THE FRENCH DEVELOP THE BRITTANY SPANIEL

In the middle years of the 1800s, the resident farmers of the Bretagne region of France began crossing some of their own spaniels with setters that had been brought in by wealthy hunters from England. Little did they realize that the breed that was to develop from these crosses would eventually impact the hunter's world around the globe.

It is important to note, however, that the English Setters of that period were most probably not the dog as we know it today. Nevertheless, it was from these crosses that took place in Bretagne that the Brittany Spaniel was to derive its name.

Just after the turn of the century Major P. Gran-Chavin, a cavalry officer and veterinarian

ORIGINS

A good many authorities doubt that spaniels originated in Spain but rather that they were taken from Wales to Spain. Those who follow this theory indicate that the spaniels then flour-ished and later spread to France, England and Scotland.

assigned to the Bretagne region of France, wrote of the many small spaniels he saw. The dogs, he said, had short tails or no tails at all and rather short ears for the spaniel breeds. He describes them as being colored white-orange, white-liver and white-black, with some tricolors as well. He also made special note of their distinctive "short gaited" movement.

At any rate, about 1910 when M. Le Comte Le Conteux de Canteleu drew up his chart of the French breeds that we find first mention of "Chien de Bretagne," the dog of Brittany. Despite its spaniel heritage, the breed was first known simply as the "Dog of Brittany" and it was not until later that the name was changed and the breed became known officially as the "Brittany Spaniel." Of course, in recent times the "Spaniel" has been omitted since

this versatile gundog breed is considered by some to be more of a pointer than a spaniel.

Much speculation exists as to which spaniel and which setter form the basis for the dog from Brittany. Attempts to determine which breeds specifically might be credited for its development are of little consequence in that the heritage of any of the spaniels of that era was questionable at best. In England, the main source of the spaniel stock, littermates often were considered different breeds depending upon how large they grew or what they looked like at maturity. To further complicate matters, the French were known to have bred their setters to some of the imported spaniels to enhance scenting ability and improve staunchness.

Eng. Ch. Mars, a dog of the early 20th century. This photo bore the caption, "That these dogs are really Setters is proved by their appearance, which closely resembles the English Setter, though the name Épagneul is used in France."

REASONS FOR TAIL DOCKING

Tail docking was performed for many reasons throughout history. Early on it was thought the practice prevented a dog from contracting the rabies virus. Another more plausible reason was that long tails could easily be injured as the dogs plunged through brush and thicket to perform their duties, whether those duties were assisting hunters or herding livestock.

An English Springer Spaniel, a breed closely related to and part of the ancestry of the Brittany.

NO TAILS

The first dog in French Spaniel history to be born without a tail is said to be the result of a cross between a French Spaniel and an English Setter. At first, this natural phenomenon was to be considered a distinctive and highly desirable trait of the breed being formed. Later, it was agreed that dogs born with tails could also be registered but their tails had to be docked close to the body.

Also popular among the French peasantry were the pointing breeds known as the Braques. It would be difficult to entirely deny the existence of the latter in the breeds that contributed to the genealogy of the Brittany Spaniel.

There is clear indication that there was at least some tendency to a very short tail or no tail at all in the initial crosses that produced the Brittany and that the colour was often white-orange or white-liver. The short tail was preferred as it was less likely to get torn by the heavy cover of the region. The more supple spaniel skin was also preferred as it lessened the likelihood of damage in the region's dense brush.

The spaniel most often credited as the cornerstone for the development of the Brittany is the Welsh Springer Spaniel. There is little doubt that spaniel blood does indeed course through the veins of today's Brittany, but to give his origin over entirely to spaniel blood would be shortsighted. Doing so would be to discount the upstanding profile and entirely un-spaniel-like character of the modern Brittany.

Although controversy may still exist as to the specific breeds used to found the basis for the Brittany, there is certainly no doubt that the end justified the means. The French produced a dog that delights all those who share their interests afield with their Brittanys, and a breed that provides great companionship for those who appreciate the breed simply for its great intelligence and enthusiastic temperament.

STANDARDIZING THE BREED
The first dogs to be shown in France that actually fit the description of the Brittany began to appear in the last decade of the

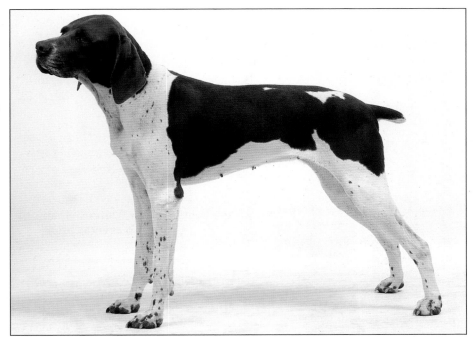

Working dogs from France classified as Braques are cited in the genealogy of the Brittany Spaniel.

LEGEND HAS IT
Legend would have us believe that the first Brittany Spaniel came about when an old French hunter and guide surreptitiously bred his liver and white female hunting dog to one of the dogs owned by a visiting English hunter. The resulting litter contained a mixture of black and white and orange and white puppies and at least one without a tail. The tailless dog proved to be a great hunter and the dog upon which the entire breed is based.

1800s. They were at first shown in a miscellaneous class open to all French Spaniels. At the same time, they participated in field trials.

Interest grew on both levels, and the development of railroads at the turn of the century gave Frenchmen an opportunity to hunt areas that were previously largely inaccessible. Interest in Brittany's own versatile spaniel grew rapidly as the hunters began to recognize both the remarkable scenting powers and the great adaptability of the breed.

In 1907 Arthur Enaud, M. de Fougeres and Dr. Gastel called a meeting at Loudeac, France to draw up a standard for their breed of choice and form a club for the advancement of the breed. Their efforts were finalized and the first Brittany Spaniel Club was formed.

Although World War I seriously crippled the efforts of many Brittany fanciers, the breed had become too popular and admired to fall into obscurity. Through the war years breeding programs, though curtailed, were carried on and the breed emerged ahead of where it had been before the war years.

THE WORD SPREADS
The Brittany was embraced and utilized on the Continent early on in the breed's development. In America acceptance was early and the Brittany earned enormous favor, fortunately among those dedicated to maintaining the breed's great ability in the field.

Although the Brittany's origin, at least in part, takes one back to British roots, acceptance was much slower in the UK. Although held in high regard among those who used the Brittany in the field, the first Field Trial Champion was not recorded until Angie Lewises' Riscoris Fleur De Lys earned the title in 1987.

The Kennel Club did not award Challenge Certificate (CC) status to Brittanys until 1997, after which time several Show Champions were made up. In 1999 Michael and Pauline Beaven's Eng. Ch. Tchao de L'Hospitaier at Brittyfull became the first "full" (field and bench) champion recorded for the breed.

Tchao was bred in Belgium by Georgine Dieck Weber and purchased by the Beavens as a puppy. He enjoyed an outstanding career in the show ring and completed his Show Championship at the 1998 Windsor Championship Show.

It is, however, the enormous immediate popularity of the breed in America and the changes that surrounded that popularity that make a brief retelling of those events noteworthy.

The first Brittany Spaniels that appeared in North America were those imported by Señor Juan Pagibet of Villa Obregon near Vera Cruz, Mexico in 1928. The next individual of note to import the breed was Louis A. Thebaud, who brought the breed to the United States in 1933. Upon Mr. Thebaud's request, the French Kennel Club sent him the Brittany Spaniel's standard of perfection in July 1934. The American Kennel Club (AKC) recognized the breed in August of that same year, but did not approve the standard until March 1935 after an acceptable translation had been completed.

America was the first country in the world not to refer to the spaniel from France as the

The versatile Brittany can be an excellent retriever in water or on land if properly trained.

Just back from a
water retrieve, all
he wants is his
owner's approval
and appreciation. A
Brittany thrives on
his owner's praise.

Brittany Spaniel. Here it is simply called the Brittany. The actual reason for the change was created by the American Brittany Club (ABC), a splinter group of the original Brittany Spaniel Club of North America (BSCNA), which had been founded in 1936. World War II all but destroyed the original club and the rapidly rising popularity of the Brittany stimulated interest in forming a new club—the ABC.

The AKC questioned the fact that "Brittany" stood alone in the club's name. The club, however, challenged the AKC's objection, stating that spaniels flushed their game and that the Brittany was a pointing dog, and not actually a true spaniel. Eventually the BSCNA and the ABC were to merge under the name of the latter and the name "Brittany" was officially adopted. The Kennel Club in Britain has also adopted this name for the French spaniel.

A MAXIMUM OF QUALITY

Gaston Pouchain, past president of the Kennel Club of France and the Brittany Spaniel Club of France, captured the essence of the breed most admirably when he described his breed as "A maximum of quality in a minimum size."

Confirming the accuracy of Pouchain's apt description is the phenomenal world-wide growth in popularity of the breed in less

than 100 years. When one stops to consider the fact that the Brittany was not breeding true to type until approximately 1910, the standardization and international acceptance are amazing.

The liver tri-color, shown here, is acceptable but not preferred in AKC shows.

There can be no doubt that dedication to dual purpose has genuinely assisted in maintaining the breed's true character. Responsible breeders continually strive to improve the conformation of the dogs they produce. However, no attempts are made to have the Brittany bred and shown for purely esthetic purposes. Thus, the hunting instinct remains foremost in the breed's character.

CHARACTERISTICS OF THE

BRITTANY

There is probably nothing quite so captivating as the comical little Brittany puppy with its wind-up toy antics and naughty little expression. If you haven't fully decided whether or not to add a Brittany puppy to your life, a visit to the home or kennel where there is a litter of puppies is probably not the best idea in the world. Anyone even thinking of dog ownership is going to be hard-pressed to resist these little charmers.

For this very reason, the person who anticipates owning a Brittany should give serious thought to the final decision. All puppies are cute—Brittany puppies are certainly no exception. All puppies are charming and seductive, but puppies are also living, breathing and very adventurous little creatures. Not only that, they depend entirely upon their human owners for everything—once they leave their mother and littermates behind.

Failure to think ahead and understand the amount of time and readjustment that dog ownership involves is one of the primary reasons that there are so many abandoned canines that end their lives in animal shelters. Buying a dog, especially a puppy, before someone is absolutely sure that they want to make that commitment can be a serious mistake.

Before a person decides to buy a dog there are some very basic conditions that must be considered. One of the first significant questions that must be answered is whether or not the person who will actually be given the responsibility

An active companion needs to be walked regularly—come rain or snow or shine!

of the dog's care actually wants a dog. This may sound like a moot point, but wanting a dog and wanting to care for it do not necessarily go hand in hand.

Children are often wildly enthusiastic about having a dog, and pets are a wonderful method of teaching children responsibility. It should be remembered, however, that childhood enthusiasm can inspire a youngster to promise anything to get what they want—but that enthusiasm may very quickly wane. Further, today's children have extremely busy schedules with school, extra-curricular activities and social events. Who will take care of the puppy once the novelty wears off? Does that person want a dog?

Desire to own a dog aside, does the lifestyle of the family actually provide for responsible dog ownership? If the entire family is away from early morning to late at night, who will provide for all of the puppy's needs?

Brittanys are wonderful with children and can keep up with the seemingly boundless energy of youngsters in the family. However, both dog and child should be supervised and taught how to treat each other with respect.

Feeding, lots of exercise time, outdoor access and the like can not be provided if no one is home.

Another important factor to consider is whether or not the breed of dog is suitable for the person or the family with which it will be living. A full-grown Brittany can handle the rough-and-tumble play of young children. A very young Brittany puppy should only be allowed playtime with young children when adults are present to supervise.

The upkeep of an adult Brittany doesn't require as much time and patience as do the luxuriously coated breeds but that does not mean the breed needs no grooming—on the contrary! Plus, the Brittany wants and needs his outdoor exercise time.

As great as claims are for a Brittany's adaptability and intelligence, remember that there is no new dog, no matter what breed, that doesn't need to be taught

MENTAL AND PHYSICAL

The Brittany's standard of perfection describes all the mental and physical characteristics that serve to produce a speedy efficient bird dog that is also a fine companion. Generations of selection on that basis give us a dog that is happiest when he is allowed to perform in that capacity.

every household rule that must be observed. Some dogs catch on more quickly than others, and puppies are just as inclined to forget or disregard lessons as are young human children.

WHY A PURE-BRED?

It is almost impossible to determine what a mixed-breed puppy will look like as an adult. More important, it may not be possible to determine what the temperament of a puppy of mixed parentage is going to be like. Will it be suitable for the person or family who wishes to own it? If the puppy grows up to be too big, too hairy or too active for the owner, what then will happen to it?

Size and temperament can vary to a degree even within pure-bred dogs. Still, controlled breeding over many generations has produced dogs giving us reasonable assurance of what a pure-bred puppy will look and act like when it reaches maturity. This predictability is more important than one might think.

Just about any dog whose background is made up of sound and healthy individuals has the potential to be a loving companion. However, the predictability of a pure-bred dog offers reasonable insurance that it will suit not only the person's esthetic demands but also the owner's lifestyle.

There is still a great deal of variation in the size of the Brittany because, relatively speaking, it is still a young breed. For example, Brittanys in the US are generally larger than the British dogs shown here.

Before you bring a Brittany puppy into your household, visit breeders and spend as much time with both puppies and adults as you can. Be sure that the adult Brittany is the dog that appeals to you both aesthetically and temperamentally.

CHARACTER

The Brittany is a gentle devoted companion, but this doesn't mean he's a "couch potato." On the contrary, this is a breed with an outgoing personality and energy to burn! The Brittany is clever to a fault and can turn on the charm in a flash, especially when he wants to get his way.

Some breeds are one-person dogs. The Brittany is best described as a "whole-family dog." A Brittany wants to be in the kitchen helping Mother with her chores and in the sitting room with the children playing games or anything else the children enjoy doing. They are glad to help the man of the household out in the garden and are excellent at plowing and planting!

Or you may find the Brittany lounging on the sofa with the elderly folks in the sitting room watching TV. This is just part of it though, for the Brittany will be ready for a day's hunt with a split second's notice. If father gets out the hunting gear—it's all business.

And when speaking of hunting, it must be clearly under-

DEVOTION

There is no doubt that the trait endearing the Brittany to so many families is its devotion to its owners. This is particularly so in regard to the children of the family. Even well-behaved toddlers find the Brittany to be a willing and patient playmate who can even be relied upon to invent games if need be.

stood that, above all, a Brittany is a hunting dog. Are there Brittanys that are bred just to be pets? Not by people who truly love the breed!

The desire and the ability to hunt are what make the Brittany unique. In the US, for example, there are in excess of 400 dual (bench and field) champions in this breed, far more than any other recognized breed. Most Brittany show dogs are hunting chums on Saturday and family show dogs on Sunday. People who love the Brittany would have it no other way.

Brittanys are listed among the most intelligent of all breeds, which is both good and bad—good in that they can learn just about anything you want to teach them and bad in that a Brittany can become bored very easily without activities that keep him busy.

As a rule, Brittanys are not a breed that can be left on their own continuously or kept outdoors alone. Their long-standing history

working alongside man in the field has made the Brittany very much a "people dog." Denied the opportunity to be with those they love, Brittanys can demand attention by developing behavior problems. Destructive digging, chewing and barking are usually signs of a bored Brittany. One of the breed's finest qualities is its desire to bond with and please its master. Not being allowed to do so can make even the best Brittany difficult to live with.

The Brittany is an ideal family dog in that he is able to share his devotion with every member of the family and has an innate ability to adjust his own mood to that of the family member he is with. He will sound the alarm to alert the family to the approach of a stranger but will be delighted to greet that same stranger if given assurance all is well.

Children always love a new puppy, especially one as appealing as a Brittany. Children must be taught to handle the puppy gently and to treat it responsibly.

TRAINABILITY

The Brittany strives to please and develops a strong bond with his owner and owner's family. Occasionally a Brittany will throw back to one of the harder ancestors in its pedigree, but by and large the breed is most amiable and, in fact, inclined to be somewhat sensitive to correction. This is not to say the breed can not withstand being corrected. Mild punishment such as a scolding or a strong "No!" accompanied by rap on the nose with a finger will not shatter the Brittany, but harsh methods can destroy the dog's personality and trainability.

Repetition and coaxing work best with the breed and, once learned, lessons seem almost a natural part of the Brittany's character. Avoidance works best. Not allowing unwanted behavior to occur in the first place is infinitely simpler than trying to convince your pup to stop something it has been doing right along.

The modern Brittany is a fantastic obedience and agility dog. But it is the breed's natural hunting ability that sells him as a breed to the hunter whether that hunter is a beginner or fully experienced. The reason for that is the Brittany always seems to know just that much more than the hunter.

There are few limits to what the breed can be trained to do. Once trained, the Brittany does not forget. A Brittany may occasionally invent new (and often better!) ways to do things but you can rely upon the Brittany to get the job done. A Brittany's nose is exceptional, which guarantees very few birds will ever escape detection. Normally he works in the same way as a Pointer but without the great range. Even at that, if greater

Training to retrieve is an enjoyable way for Brittanys to exercise their bodies and minds. The breed's working instincts and innate skills make them naturals at it!

range and speed are desired, a Brittany pup can be purchased from a line that is from field-trial stock versus hunting/show stock.

The Brittany points and holds his game. He retrieves on both land and water, although he must be protected after water retrieving in freezing weather. Brittanys do not have the double, oil-enhanced coat or fat layer of the retrievers. The Brittany is a breed that can be used for both fur and feather.

BRITTANYS AND THE WORLD AT LARGE

Brittanys love their own people and their normally happy-go-lucky manner belies a protective instinct that emerges when danger threatens. Although most gundogs are not thought of as having protective instincts, the Brittany will rise to the cause if required. It should be understood that this protective nature is reserved for the family. When it comes to property, most Brittanys could not care less if an intruder set about removing every piece of furniture in the house (unless of course it was their favorite chair!).

This is not to say a Brittany would also hop into the intruder's truck as part of the spoils. When it comes to strangers, Brits can run the gamut. A good deal depends upon the degree of socialization the individual is given but even at that, some members of the breed are

HIGH-ENERGY
The Brittany has an extremely high-energy level and some consider this to be a "hyper" or "frenetic" personality. This is not the case if the Brittany is given sufficient exercise and attention. In fact, most Brittanys take time out from their roles as household companions to take on a starring role as bird dog par excellence.

delighted to meet everyone who comes along and offers a kind word or pat on the head. Others may not be demonstrative at all and some Brittanys would be just as happy if they didn't have to deal with outsiders at all.

DO YOU KNOW ABOUT HIP DYSPLASIA?

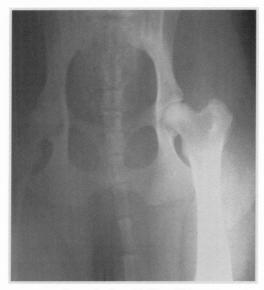

X-ray of a dog with "Good" hips.

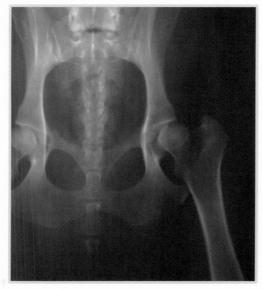

X-ray of a dog with "Moderate" dysplastic hips.

Hip dysplasia is a fairly common condition found in pure-bred dogs. When a dog has hip dysplasia, his hind leg has an incorrectly formed hip joint. By constant use of the hip joint, it becomes more and more loose, wears abnormally and may become arthritic.

Hip dysplasia can only be confirmed with an x-ray, but certain symptoms may indicate a problem. Your dog may have a hip dysplasia problem if he walks in a peculiar manner, hops instead of smoothly runs, uses his hind legs in unison (to keep the pressure off the weak joint), has trouble getting up from a prone position or always sits with both legs together on one side of his body. As the dog matures, he may adapt well to life with a bad hip, but in a few years the arthritis develops and many dogs with hip dysplasia become crippled.

Hip dysplasia is considered an inherited disease and only can be diagnosed definitively by x-ray when the dog is two years old, although symptoms often appear earlier. Some experts claim that a special diet might help your puppy outgrow the bad hip, but the usual treatments are surgical. The removal of the pectineus muscle, the removal of the round part of the femur, reconstructing the pelvis and replacing the hip with an artificial one are all surgical interventions that are expensive, but they are usually very successful. Follow the advice of your veterinarian.

They are much the same with other dogs and animals. Some Brittanys are a bit reserved when strange dogs approach, others know no enemies in the canine world. Most properly raised Brittanys are happy to co-exist with any other four-legged family pet that might share the home.

Winged pets will have little problem with a Brittany as long as the birds are confined to their cages. Everything in a Brittany's genetic makeup tells the dog something must be done about birds, and it will take a good deal of restraint for the Brit to remain calm and indifferent with the family parakeet or canary flitting about the room.

HEALTH CONCERNS

Considering the Brittany's triple-threat popularity in the home, field and show ring, the breed is not plagued with a preponderance of the hereditary health problems found in so many other breeds. Certainly a contributing factor is the breed's natural and efficient conformation. The breed standard calls for no exaggerated physical characteristics.

It is not the least bit unusual to have the well-cared-for Brittany live to be 12 to 13 years of age, acting hale and hearty. If there is anything that breeders watch closely it would be hip dysplasia, a problem that seems to plague practically all breeds.

Hip dysplasia is a condition in which the ball and socket arrangement of the hip and upper femur is so poorly developed that the femur rotates within the socket. Depending upon the severity of the condition, hip dysplasia can cause stiffness and limping or even total paralysis of the rear quarters.

Corrective surgery has been perfected but, needless to say, with an active, versatile dog like the Brittany it makes sense to seek out a breeder who screens their breeding stock and does their best to avoid using affected animals in their breeding programs.

Some cases of epilepsy have been reported in the breed. Here again, however, discussing the problem with the breeder from whom you buy your puppy will relieve your mind of the frequency, if any, in the breeder's line.

TAKING CARE

Science is showing that as people take care of their pets, the pets are taking care of their owners. A recent study published in the *American Journal of Cardiology*, found that having a pet can prolong his owner's life. Pet owners generally have lower blood pressure, and pets help their owners to relax and keep more physically fit. It was also found that pets help to keep the elderly connected to their communities.

BRITTANY

In the earliest days of man's relationship with dogs, he began to see that those particular dogs constructed in a certain way were more successful at performing the tasks assigned to them. It then became those particular characteristics that guided man's breeding practices.

The people who kept the dogs that were serving them best gathered to make comparisons and seek out stock to improve their own lines. The more successful keepers were asked to observe the dogs at work and evaluate them.

With industrialization, little villages grew into large cities and towns and the citizenry moved into urban dwellings. Fewer and fewer dogs were given the opportunity to perform in the capacity for which their breed was created. To avoid the respective breeds' losing their ability to perform, dog fanciers began to select their stock on the basis of the conformation they determined would produce the most successful workers. The guidelines or standards became theoretical rather than practical.

In many cases the accent that had previously been on function was now placed on form. It should be easy to see, once form was the keynote, how breeds whose only purpose was to be esthetically pleasing would gain an equal place of respect alongside their working relatives.

It should be noted here that these descriptions were the forerunners of breed standards and that they were written by knowledgeable individuals in the breed for their peers. They were

The Brittany's general appearance should be that of a closely knit, compact and lively dog, according to the breed standard.

all thoroughly familiar with their breeds. The descriptions were used primarily as checklists or blueprints to breed by, and they served as reminders so that important points of conformation would not be lost.

It should be understood, however, that not all fanciers neglected the original purpose of their breeds. For example, devotees of the Brittany have been adamant in maintaining those characteristics that enable our breed to excel as a hunter.

Today's Brittany standard describes the ideal hunting dog. It was written by individuals versed in the breed's type and ability in the field. It includes a description of ideal structure, temperament, coat, color and the manner in which the breed moves. All of these descriptions are based upon what constitutes an efficient hunter and reliable companion.

Standards are used by breeders to assist them in breeding toward this goal of perfection. While no dog is absolutely perfect, the dogs that adhere closest to the ideal are what breeders will determine is show or breeding stock, and the dogs that deviate to any great extent are considered companion or pet stock.

The standard is also used by dog show judges to compare actual dogs to the ideal. The dog adhering closest to this ideal is then the winner of the class and so on down the line.

THE AMERICAN KENNEL CLUB STANDARD FOR THE BRITTANY

General Appearance: A compact, closely knit dog of medium size, a leggy dog having the appearance, as well as the agility, of a great ground coverer. Strong, vigorous, energetic and quick of movement. Ruggedness, without clumsiness, is a characteristic of the breed. He can be tailless or has a tail docked to approximately 4 inches.

Size, Proportion, Substance: *Height*—17.5 to 20.5 inches, measured from the ground to the highest point of the shoulders. Any Brittany measuring under 17.5 inches or over 20.5 inches shall be disqualified from dog show competition. *Weight*— Should weigh between 30 and 40 pounds. *Proportion*— So leggy is he that his height at the shoulders is the same as the length of his body. *Body Length*— Approximately the same as the height when measured at the shoulders. Body length is measured from the point of the forechest to the rear of the rump. A long body should be heavily penalized. *Substance*—Not too light in bone, yet never heavy-boned and cumbersome.

Head: *Expression*—Alert and eager, but with the soft expression of a bird dog. *Eyes*—Well set in head. Well protected from briars by a heavy, expressive eyebrow. A prominent full or popeye should be penalized. It is a serious fault in a dog that must face briars. Skull well chiseled under the eyes, so that the lower lid is not pulled back to form a pocket or haw that would catch seeds, dirt and weed dust. Preference should be for the darker colored eyes, though lighter shades of amber should not be penalized. Light and mean-looking eyes should be heavily penalized. *Ears*—Set high, above the level of the eyes. Short and triangular, rather than pendulous, reaching about half the length of the muzzle. Should lie flat and close to the head, with

A dog in profile showing correct balance, type, substance, structure and coat.

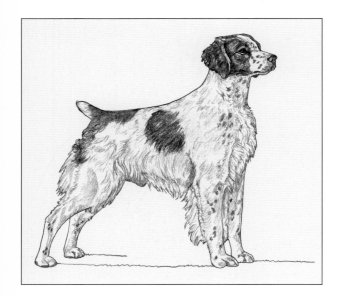

dense, but relatively short hair, and with little fringe. *Skull*—Medium length, rounded, very slightly wedge-shaped, but evenly made. Width, not quite as wide as the length and never so broad as to appear coarse, or so narrow as to appear racy. Well defined, but gently sloping stop. Median line rather indistinct. The occiput only apparent to the touch. Lateral walls well rounded. The Brittany should never be "apple-headed" and he should never have an indented stop. *Muzzle*—Medium length, about two-thirds the length of the skull, measuring the muzzle from the tip to the stop, and the skull from the occiput to the stop. Muzzle should taper gradually in both horizontal and vertical dimensions as it approaches the nostrils. Neither a Roman nose nor a dish-face is desirable. Never broad, heavy or snippy. *Nose*—Nostrils well open to permit deep breathing of air and adequate scenting. Tight nostrils should be penalized. Never shiny. Color: fawn, tan, shades of brown or deep pink. A black nose is a disqualification. A two-tone or butterfly nose should be penalized. *Lips*—Tight, the upper lip overlapping the lower jaw just to cover the lower lip. Lips dry, so that feathers will not stick. Drooling to be heavily penalized. Flews to be penalized. *Bite*—A true scissors bite. Overshot or undershot jaw to be heavily penalized.

Neck, Topline, Body: *Neck*—
Medium length. Free from throatiness, though not a serious fault unless accompanied by dewlaps, strong without giving the impression of being over muscled. Well set into sloping shoulders. Never concave or ewe-necked. *Topline*—Slight slope from the highest point of the shoulders to the root of the tail. *Chest*—Deep, reaching the level of the elbow. Neither so wide nor so rounded as to disturb the placement of the shoulders and elbows. Ribs well sprung. Adequate heart room provided by depth as well as width. Narrow or slab-sided chests are a fault. *Back*—Short and straight. Never hollow, saddle, sway or roach backed. Slight drop from the hips to the root of the tail. *Flanks*—Rounded. Fairly full. Not extremely tucked up, or flabby and falling. Loins short and strong. Distance from last rib to upper thigh short, about three to four fingers' widths. Narrow and weak loins are a fault. In motion, the loin should not sway sideways, giving a zig-zag motion to the back, wasting energy. *Tail*—Tailless to approximately 4 inches, natural or docked. The tail not to be so long as to affect the overall balance of the dog. Set on high, actually an extension of the spine at about the same level. Any tail substantially more than four inches shall be severely penalized.

Brittany showing a head of correct type, balance and structure.

Forequarters: *Shoulders*—
Shoulder blades should not protrude too much, not too wide apart, with perhaps two thumbs' width between. Sloping and muscular. Blade and upper arm should form nearly a 90-degree angle. Straight shoulders are a fault. At the shoulders, the Brittany is slightly higher than at the rump. *Front Legs*—Viewed from the front, perpendicular, but not set too wide. Elbows and feet turning neither in nor out. Pasterns slightly sloped. Down in pasterns is a serious fault. Leg bones clean, graceful, but not too fine. Extremely heavy bone is as much a fault as spindly legs. One must look for substance and suppleness. Height at elbows should approximately equal distance from elbow to withers. *Feet*—Should be strong, propor-

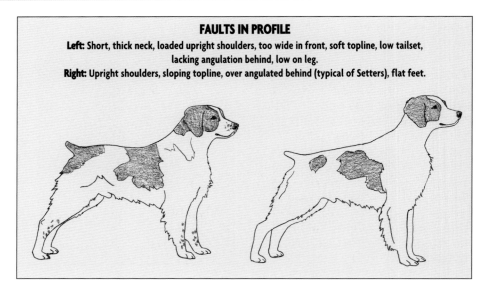

FAULTS IN PROFILE

Left: Short, thick neck, loaded upright shoulders, too wide in front, soft topline, low tailset, lacking angulation behind, low on leg.

Right: Upright shoulders, sloping topline, over angulated behind (typical of Setters), flat feet.

tionately smaller than the spaniels', with close fitting, well arched toes and thick pads. The Brittany is "not up on his toes." Toes not heavily feathered. Flat feet, splayed feet, paper feet, etc., are to be heavily penalized. An ideal foot is halfway between the hare and the cat foot. Dewclaws may be removed.

Hindquarters: Broad strong and muscular, with powerful thighs and well bent stifles, giving the angulation necessary for powerful drive. *Hind Legs*—Stifles well bent. The stifle should not be so angulated as to place the hock joint far out behind the dog. A Brittany should not be condemned for straight stifle until the judge has checked the dog in motion from the side. The stifle joint should not

turn out making a cowhock. Thighs well feathered but not profusely, halfway to the hock. Hocks, that is, the back pasterns, should be moderately short, pointing neither in nor out, perpendicular when viewed from the side. They should be firm when shaken by the judge. *Feet*—Same as front feet.

Coat: Dense, flat or wavy, never curly. Texture neither wiry nor silky. Ears should carry little fringe. The front and hind legs should have some feathering, but too little is definitely preferable to too much. Dogs with long or profuse feathering or furnishings shall be so severely penalized as to effectively eliminate them from competition. *Skin*— Fine and fairly loose. A loose skin rolls with briars and sticks, thus diminishing punctures or tearing. A skin so loose as to form pouches is undesirable.

Color: Orange and white or liver and white in either clear or roan patterns. Some ticking is desirable. The orange or liver is found in the standard parti-color or piebald patterns. Washed out colors are not desirable. Tri-colors are allowed but not preferred. A tri-color is a liver and white dog with classic orange markings on eyebrows, muzzle and cheeks, inside the ears and under the tail, freckles on the lower legs are orange. Anything exceeding the limits of these markings shall be severely penalized. Black is a disqualification.

Gait: When at a trot the Brittany's hind foot should step into or beyond the print left by the front foot. Clean movement, coming and going, is very important, but most important is side gait, which is smooth, efficient and ground covering.

Temperament: A happy, alert dog, neither mean nor shy.

Disqualifications Any Brittany measuring under 17.5 inches or over 20.5 inches. A black nose. Black in the coat.

Approved April 10, 1990
Effective May 31, 1990

FAULTS IN PROFILE

Left: Ewe-necked, upright shoulders, weak pasterns, low on leg, soft topline, low tail set, lacking angulation behind, long back.
Right: Thick neck, loaded shoulders, wide front, flat feet, lacking angulation in rear.

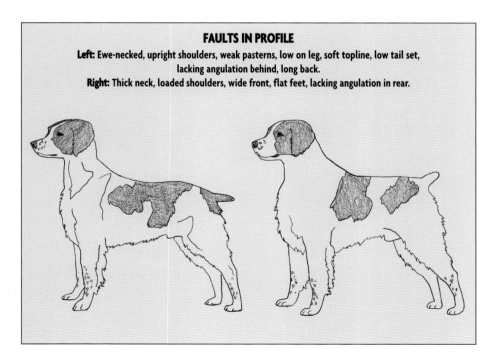

BRITTANY

HOW TO SELECT
A BRITTANY PUPPY

Your Brittany should only be purchased from a breeder who has earned a reputation for consistently producing dogs that are mentally and physically sound. The only way a breeder can earn this reputation is through selective breeding aimed at eliminating genetic weaknesses.

The first question a prospective owner should ask a breeder is, "What is the most important quality you breed for?" Deal only with those breeders who put good temperament and good health above all else.

Another important question to ask is what the breeder does with his Brittanys. Does he hunt his dogs or compete in field trials? Are the dogs shown in conformation competition or in obedience? If the person you are talking to breeds Brittanys only to sell, go somewhere else for your dog!

Remember that the puppy you select will grow up to be a part of your family for years to come, so take your time in making the selection. Do some research and use your head, not just your heart.

Cleanliness in both the dogs and the areas in which the dogs are kept is a bottom-line requirement, so take note of these. This is the first clue that tells you how much the breeder cares about the dogs he raises.

The Brittany puppy you buy should be a happy and bouncy extrovert. However, if you are not going to be hunting with your Brittany and just want a companion, you need not necessarily select the leader of the little pack. The extremely bold and extroverted pup will undoubtedly demand a lot more exercise and attention to keep him wound down than his littermates. This does not mean you should select a shy, shrinking-violet puppy. This is not typical of correct Brittany attitude.

Healthy Brittany puppies are strong and firm to the touch, never bony or, on the other hand, obese and bloated. Coats will be lustrous with no sign of dry or flaky skin. The inside of the puppy's ears should be pink and clean. Dark discharge or a bad odor could indicate ear mites, a sure sign of poor maintenance. The healthy Brittany puppy's breath smells sweet. The teeth are clean and white and there should never be any malformation of the mouth or jaw. The puppy's eyes should be clear and bright. Eyes that appear runny and irritated indicate serious problems.

SHOULD YOU BUY A MALE OR FEMALE BRITTANY?

The Brittany is one breed in which, outside size and a bit of difference in the amount of coat, there isn't a great number of sex-related differences. The choice is primarily the buyer's.

If you have decided upon the sex of the puppy you want, stand by your choice and do not have someone change your mind because that is "all that is left."

Females do have their semi-annual heat cycles once they have passed nine or ten months of age. During these heat cycles of approximately 21 days, she must be confined to avoid soiling her surroundings with the bloody discharge that accompanies estrus. She must also be carefully watched to prevent males from gaining access to her or she will become pregnant.

Owners of some other breeds find training males not to "lift their legs" and mark their territory somewhat difficult. Brittany males are not difficult to correct in this respect. A Brittany male can get "the urge to travel" if not kept active and interested at home. Males are not beyond turning their attention toward "thoughts of love," particularly if the female Poodle or Golden Retriever down the road is having her heat period.

Nearly all sexually related problems can be avoided by having the pet Brittany "altered." Spaying the female and neutering the male saves the pet owner all the headaches of sexually related problems without changing the character of the breed.

There should be no sign of discharge from the nose nor should it ever be crusted or runny. Coughing and diarrhea are danger signals as are any eruptions on the skin. The coat should be soft and lustrous.

The healthy Brittany puppy's front legs should be straight as little posts. Even at an early age, a Brittany puppy's legs appear long in proportion. Movement is light and bouncy and true.

ARE YOU PREPARED?

Unfortunately, when a puppy is bought by someone who does not take into consideration the time and attention that dog ownership requires, it is the puppy who suffers when he is either abandoned or placed in a shelter by a frustrated owner. So all of the "homework" you do in preparation for your pup's arrival will benefit you both. The more informed you are, the more you will know what to expect and the better equipped you will be to handle the ups and downs of raising a puppy.

Hopefully, everyone in the household is willing to do his part in raising and caring for the pup. The anticipation of owning a dog often brings a lot of promises from excited family members: "I will walk him every day," "I will feed him," "I will house-train him," etc., but these things take time and effort, and promises can easily be forgotten once the novelty of the new pet has worn off.

It should be understood that the most any breeder can offer is an opinion on the "show potential" of a particular puppy. Any predictions breeders make about puppies' future are based upon their experience with past litters that have produced winning show dogs. It is obvious that the more successful a breeder has been in producing winning Brittanys over the years, the broader his base of comparison will be. Give serious consideration to both what the standard says a correct Brittany must look like and what the breeder's recommendations are.

COMMITMENT OF OWNERSHIP

Researching your breed, selecting a responsible breeder and observing as many pups as possible are all important steps on the way to dog ownership. It may seem like a lot of effort...and you have not even taken the pup home yet! Remember, though, you cannot be too careful when it comes to deciding on the type of dog you want and finding out about your prospective pup's background. Buying a puppy is not—or should not be—just another whimsical purchase. This is one instance in which you actually do get to choose your own family! You may be thinking that buying a puppy should be fun—it should not be so serious and so much work. Keep in mind that your puppy is not a cuddly stuffed toy or decorative lawn ornament, but a creature that will become a real member of your family. You will come to realize that, while buying a puppy is a pleasurable and exciting endeavor, it is not something to be taken lightly. Relax…the fun will start when the pup comes home!

Always keep in mind that a puppy is nothing more than a baby in a furry disguise…a baby who is virtually helpless in a human world and who trusts his owner for fulfillment of his basic needs for survival. In addition to food, water and shelter, your pup needs care, protection, guidance and love. If you are not prepared to commit to this, then you are not ready to own a dog.

"Wait a minute," you say. "How hard could this be? All of my neighbors own dogs and they seem to be doing just fine. Why

TEMPERAMENT COUNTS

Your selection of a good puppy can be determined by your needs. A show potential, a hunter or a good pet? It is your choice. Every puppy, however, should be of good temperament. Although show-quality puppies are bred and raised with emphasis on physical conformation, responsible breeders strive for equally good temperament. Do not buy from a breeder who concentrates solely on physical beauty at the expense of personality and soundness.

should I have to worry about all of this?" Well, you should not worry about it; in fact, you will probably find that once your Brittany pup gets used to his new home, he will fall into his place in the family quite naturally. But it never hurts to emphasize the

that could be your most loyal friend.

PREPARING PUPPY'S PLACE IN YOUR HOME

Researching your breed and finding a breeder are only two aspects of the homework you will have to do before taking your Brittany puppy home. You will also have to prepare your home and family for the new addition. Much as you would prepare a nursery for a newborn baby, you will need to designate a place in your home that will be the puppy's own. How you prepare your home will depend on how much freedom the dog will be allowed. Whatever you

PUPPY PERSONALITY

When a litter becomes available to you, choosing a pup out of all of those adorable faces will not be an easy task! Sound temperament is of utmost importance, but each pup has his own personality and some may be better suited to you than others. A feisty, independent pup will do well in a home with older children and adults, while quiet, shy puppies will thrive in homes with minimal noise and distractions. Your breeder knows the pups best and should be able to guide you in the right direction.

What could be more exciting than bringing home a new Brittany puppy? Bringing home two is at least twice as exciting.

commitment of dog ownership. With some time and patience, it is really not too difficult to raise a curious and exuberant Brittany pup to be a well-adjusted and well-mannered adult dog—a dog

decide, you must ensure that he has a place that he can "call his own."

When you bring your new puppy into your home, you are bringing him into what will become his home as well. Obviously, you did not buy a puppy so that he could rule the roost, but in order for a puppy to grow into a stable, well-adjusted dog, he has to feel comfortable in his surroundings. Remember, he is leaving the warmth and security of his mother and littermates, as well as the familiarity of the only place he has ever known, so it is important to make his transition as easy as possible. By preparing a place in your home for the puppy, you are making him feel as welcome as possible in a strange new place. It should not take him long to get used to it, but the sudden shock of being transplanted is somewhat traumatic for a young pup. Imagine how a small child would feel in the same situation—that is how your puppy must be feeling. It is up to you to reassure him and to let him know, "Little fellow, you are going to like it here!"

WHAT YOU SHOULD BUY

CRATE

To someone unfamiliar with the use of crates in dog training, it

may seem like punishment to shut a dog in a crate, but this is not the case at all. Most experienced breeders and trainers recommend crates as preferred tools for show puppies as well as pet puppies. Crates are not cruel—crates have many humane and highly effective uses in dog care and training. For example, crate training is a very popular and very successful

All puppies are curious and love to explore. Provide your pup with plenty of safe diversions and careful super-vision.

PUPPY APPEARANCE
Your puppy should have a well-fed appearance but not a distended abdomen, which may indicate worms or incorrect feeding, or both. The body should be firm, with a solid feel. The skin of the abdomen should be pale pink and clean, without signs of scratching or rash. Check the fore and hind legs to make certain that dewclaws were removed, though this is optional for this breed.

PEDIGREE VS. REGISTRATION CERTIFICATE

Too often new owners are confused between these two important docu- ments. Your puppy's pedigree, essen- tially a family tree, is a written record of a dog's genealogy of three genera- tions or more. The pedigree will show you the names as well as performance titles of all dogs in your pup's back- ground. Your breeder must provide you with a registration application, with his part properly filled out. You must complete the application and send it to the AKC with the proper fee. Every puppy must come from a litter that has been AKC-registered by the breeder, born in the US and from a sire and dam that are also registered with the AKC.

The seller must provide you with complete records to identify the puppy. The AKC requires that the seller provide the buyer with the following: breed; sex, color and mark- ings; date of birth; litter number (when available); names and registra- tion numbers of the parents; breeder's name; and date sold or delivered.

house-training method. A crate can keep your dog safe during travel and, perhaps most importantly, a crate provides your dog with a place of his own in your home. It serves as a "doggie bedroom" of sorts—your Brittany can curl up in his crate when he wants to sleep or when

he just needs a break. Many dogs sleep in their crates overnight. With soft bedding and his favorite toy, a crate becomes a cozy pseudo-den for your dog. Like his ancestors, he too will seek out the comfort and retreat of a den—you just happen to be providing him with something a little more luxurious than what his early ancestors enjoyed.

As far as purchasing a crate, the type that you buy is up to you. It will most likely be one of the two most popular types: wire or fiberglass. There are advantages and disadvantages to each type. For example, a wire crate is more open, allowing the air to flow through and affording the dog a view of what is going on around him while a fiberglass crate is sturdier. Both can double

PET INSURANCE

Just like you can insure your car, your house and your own health, you likewise can insure your dog's health. Investigate a pet insurance policy by talking to your vet. Depending on the age of your dog, the breed and the kind of coverage you desire, your policy can be very affordable. Most policies cover accidental injuries, poisoning and thousands of medical problems and illnesses, including cancers. Some carriers also offer routine care and immunization coverage.

as travel crates, providing protection for the dog. The size of the crate is another thing to consider. Puppies do not stay puppies forever—in fact, sometimes it seems as if they grow right before your eyes. A small crate may be fine for a very young Brittany pup, but it will not do him much good for long! Since you want your Brittany to accept his crate as his own space, it is better to get one that will accommodate your dog both as a pup and at full size. A medium-size crate will be necessary for a full-grown Brittany, who stands approximately 20 inches high.

BEDDING

A soft crate pad in the dog's crate will help the dog feel more at home, and you may also like to give him in a small blanket. This will take the place of the

PHOTO COURTESY OF DOSKOUL

leaves, twigs, etc., that the pup would use in the wild to make a den; the pup can make his own "burrow" in the crate. Although your pup is far removed from his den-making ancestors, the denning instinct is still a part of his genetic makeup. Second, until you take your pup home, he has been sleeping amid the warmth of his dam and littermates, and while a blanket is not the same as a warm, breathing body, it still provides heat and something with which to snuggle. You will want to wash your pup's bedding frequently in case he has an accident in his crate, and replace or remove any blanket that becomes ragged and starts to fall apart.

Toys

Toys are a must for dogs of all ages, especially for curious playful pups. Puppies are the "children" of the dog world, and what child does not love toys? Chew toys provide enjoyment for both dog and owner—your dog will enjoy playing with his favorite toys, while you will enjoy the fact that they distract him from your expensive shoes and leather sofa. Puppies love to chew; in fact, chewing is a physical need for pups as they are teething, and everything looks appetizing! The full range of your possessions—from old glove to Oriental carpet—are fair game in the eyes of a teething pup. Puppies are not all that discerning when it comes to finding something to literally "sink their teeth into"—everything tastes great!

Brittany puppies are fairly aggressive chewers and only the hardest, strongest toys should be offered to them. Breeders advise owners to resist stuffed toys, because they can become de-stuffed in no time. The overly excited pup may ingest the

CRATE-TRAINING TIPS

During crate training, you should partition off the section of the crate in which the pup stays. If he is given too big an area, this will hinder your training efforts. Crate training is based on the fact that a dog does not like to soil his sleeping quarters, so it is ineffective to keep a pup in an area that is so big that he can eliminate in one end and get far enough away from it to sleep. Also, you want to make the crate den-like for the pup. Blankets and a favorite toy will make the crate cozy for the small pup; as he grows, you may want to evict some of his "roommates" to make more room. It will take some coaxing at first, but be patient. Given some time to get used to it, your pup will adapt to his new home-within-a-home quite nicely.

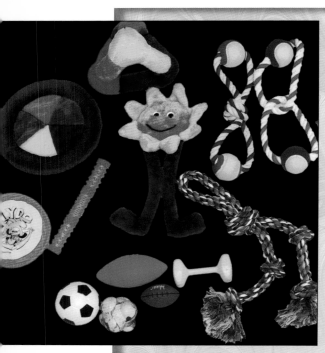

TOYS, TOYS, TOYS!

With a big variety of dog toys available, and so many that look like they would be a lot of fun for a dog, be careful in your selection. It is amazing what a set of puppy teeth can do to an innocent-looking toy, so, obviously, safety is a major consideration. Be sure to choose the most durable products that you can find. Hard nylon bones and toys are a safe bet, and many of them are offered in different scents and flavors that will be sure to capture your dog's attention. It is always fun to play a game of fetch with your dog, and there are balls and flying discs that are specially made to withstand dog teeth.

In addition to his crate, your Brittany may enjoy a soft dog bed in which he can cuddle up.

stuffing, which is neither digestible nor nutritious.

Similarly, squeaky toys are quite popular, but must be avoided for the Brittany. Perhaps a squeaky toy can be used as an aid in training, but not for free play. If a pup "disembowels" one of these, the small plastic squeaker inside can be dangerous if swallowed. Monitor the condition of all your pup's toys carefully and get rid of any that have been chewed to the point of becoming potentially dangerous.

Be careful of natural bones, which have a tendency to splinter into sharp, dangerous pieces. Also be careful of rawhide, which can turn into pieces that are easy to swallow and become a mushy mess on your carpet.

LEAD

A nylon lead is probably the best option as it is the most resistant to puppy teeth should your pup

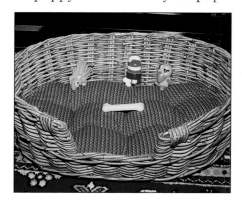

take a liking to chewing on his lead. Of course, this is a habit that should be nipped in the bud, but if your pup likes to chew on his lead he has a very slim chance of being able to chew through the strong nylon. Nylon leads are also lightweight, which is good for a young Brittany who is just getting used to the idea of walking on a lead. For everyday walking and safety purposes, the nylon lead is a good choice. As your pup grows up and gets used to walking on the lead, you may want to purchase a flexible lead. These leads allow you to extend the length to give the dog a broader area to explore or to shorten the length to keep the dog near you. Of course there are special leads for training purposes, and specially made leather harnesses, but these are not necessary for routine walks.

COLLAR

Your pup should get used to wearing a collar every day since you will want to attach his ID tags to it. Plus, you have to attach the lead to something! A lightweight nylon collar is a good choice; make sure that it fits snugly enough so that the pup cannot wriggle out of it, but is loose enough so that it will not be uncomfortably tight around the pup's neck. You should be able to fit a finger

MENTAL AND DENTAL
Toys not only help your puppy get the physical and mental stimulation he needs but also provide a great way to keep his teeth clean. Hard rubber or nylon toys, especially those con- structed with grooves, are designed to scrape away plaque, preventing bad breath and gum infection.

between the pup and the collar. It may take some time for your pup to get used to wearing the collar, but soon he will not even notice that it is there. Choke collars are made for training, but should only be used by an experienced handler.

FOOD AND WATER BOWLS

Your pup will need two bowls, one for food and one for water. You may want two sets of bowls, one for inside and one for outside, depending on where the dog will be fed and where he will be spending time. Stainless steel or sturdy plastic bowls are popular choices. Plastic bowls are more chewable. Dogs tend not to chew on the steel variety, which can be sterilized. It is important to buy sturdy bowls since anything is in danger of being chewed by puppy

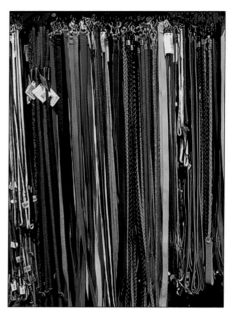

FINANCIAL RESPONSIBILITY
Grooming tools, collars, leashes, crate, dog beds and, of course, toys will be expenses to you when you first obtain your pup, and the cost will continue throughout your dog's lifetime. If your puppy damages or destroys your possessions (as most puppies surely will!) or something belonging to a neighbor, you can calculate additional expense. There is also flea and pest control, which every dog owner faces more than once. You must be able to handle the financial responsibility of owning a dog.

teeth and you do not want your dog to be constantly chewing apart his bowl (for his safety and for your purse!).

CLEANING SUPPLIES
Until your pup is house-trained, you will be doing a lot of cleaning. Accidents will occur, which is acceptable in the beginning because the puppy does not know any better. All you can do is be prepared to clean up any accidents. Old rags, towels, newspapers and a safe disinfectant are good to have on hand.

BEYOND THE BASICS
The items previously discussed are the bare necessities. You will find out what else you need as

CHOOSE AN APPROPRIATE COLLAR

The **BUCKLE COLLAR** is the standard collar used for everyday purposes. Be sure that you adjust the buckle on growing puppies. Check it every day. It can become too tight overnight! These collars can be made of leather or nylon. Attach your dog's identification tags to this collar.

The **CHOKE COLLAR** is the usual collar recommended for training. It is constructed of highly polished steel so that it slides easily through the stainless steel loop. The idea is that the dog controls the pressure around its neck and he will stop pulling if the collar becomes uncomfortable. Never leave a choke collar on your dog when not training.

The **HALTER** is for a trained dog that has to be restrained to prevent running away, chasing a cat and the like. Considered the most humane of all collars, it is frequently used on smaller dogs for which collars are not comfortable.

Your local pet shop sells an array of dishes and bowls for water and food.

PHOTO COURTESY OF MIKKI PET PRODUCTS.

you go along—grooming supplies, flea/tick protection, baby gates to partition a room, etc. These things will vary depending on your situation but it is important that you have everything you need to feed and make your Brittany comfortable in his first few days at home.

PUPPY-PROOFING YOUR HOME

Aside from making sure that your Brittany will be comfortable in your home, you also have to make sure that your home is safe for your Brittany. This means taking precautions that your pup will not get into anything he should not get into and that there is nothing within his reach that may harm him should he sniff it, chew it, inspect it, etc. This probably seems obvious since, while you are primarily concerned with your pup's safety, at the same time you do not want your belongings to be

SKULL & CROSSBONES
Thoroughly puppy-proof your house before bringing your puppy home. Never use cockroach or rodent poisons or plant fertilizers in any area accessible to the puppy. Avoid the use of toilet cleaners. Most dogs are born with "toilet-bowl sonar" and will take a drink if the lid is left open. Also keep the trash secured and out of reach.

CHEMICAL TOXINS

Scour your garage for potential puppy dangers. Remove weed killers, pesticides and antifreeze materials. Antifreeze is highly toxic and just a few drops can kill a puppy or an adult dog. The sweet taste attracts the animal, who will quickly consume it from the floor or pavement.

It is your responsibility to clean up after your dog has relieved himself. Pet shops have various aids to assist you in the cleanup job.

ruined. Breakables should be placed out of reach if your dog is to have full run of the house. If he is to be limited to certain places within the house, keep any potentially dangerous items in the "off-limits" areas. An electrical cord can pose a danger should the puppy decide to taste it—and who is going to convince a pup that it would not make a great chew toy? Cords should be fastened tightly against the wall. If your dog is going to spend time in a crate, make sure that there is nothing near his crate that he can reach if he sticks his curious little nose or paws through the openings. Just as you would with a child, keep all household cleaners and chemicals where the pup cannot reach them.

It is also important to make sure that the outside of your home is safe. Of course your puppy should never be unsupervised, but a pup let loose in the yard will want to run and explore, and he should be granted that freedom. Do not let a fence give you a false sense of security; you would be surprised how crafty (and persistent) a dog can be in working out how to dig under and squeeze his way through small holes, or to jump

Puppies don't discriminate when it comes to chewing! There's no accounting for puppies' tastes when it comes to something to chomp on.

TOXIC PLANTS

If you see your dog carrying a piece of vegetation in his mouth, approach him in a quiet, disinterested manner, avoid eye contact, pet him and gradually remove the plant from his mouth. Alternatively, offer him a treat and maybe he'll drop the plant on his own accord. Be sure no toxic plants are growing in your own yard or kept in your home.

or climb over a fence. The remedy is to make the fence well embedded into the ground and high enough so that it really is impossible for your dog to get over it (about 6 feet should suffice). Be sure to repair or secure any gaps in the fence. Check the fence periodically to ensure that it is in good shape and make repairs as needed; a very determined pup may return to the same spot to "work on it" until he is able to get through.

FIRST TRIP TO THE VET

You have selected your puppy, and your home and family are ready. Now all you have to do is collect your Brittany from the breeder and the fun begins, right? Well...not so fast. Something else you need to prepare is your pup's first trip to the veterinarian. Perhaps the breeder can recommend someone in the area who specializes in hunting breeds, or maybe you know some other Brittany owners who can suggest a good vet. Either way, you should have an appointment arranged for your pup before you pick him up.

The pup's first visit will consist of an overall examination to make sure that the pup does not have any problems that are not apparent to you. The veterinarian will also set up a schedule for the pup's vaccinations; the breeder will inform you of which ones the pup has already received and the vet can continue from there.

INTRODUCTION TO THE FAMILY

Everyone in the house will be excited about the puppy's coming home and will want to pet him and play with him, but it is best to make the introduction low-key so as not to overwhelm the puppy. He is apprehensive already. It is the first time he has been separated from his dam and the breeder, and the ride to your home is likely to be the first time he has been in a car. The last thing you want to do is smother him, as this will only frighten him further. This is not to say that human contact is not extremely necessary at this stage, because this is the time when a connection between the pup and his human family is formed. Gentle petting and soothing

NATURAL TOXINS

Examine your grass and landscaping before bringing your puppy home. Many varieties of plants have leaves, stems or flowers that are toxic if ingested, and you can depend on a curious puppy to investigate them. Ask your vet for information on poisonous plants or research them at your library.

words should help console him, as well as just putting him down and letting him explore on his own (under your watchful eye, of course).

The pup may approach the family members or may busy himself with exploring for a while. Gradually, each person should spend some time with the pup, one at a time, crouching down to get as close to the pup's

Life is filled with many colorful, good-smelling experiences. Keep your Brittany pup happy and safe and away from unknown plants.

level as possible and letting him sniff their hands and petting him gently. He definitely needs human attention and he needs to be touched—this is how to form an immediate bond. Just remember that the pup is experiencing a lot of things for the first time, at the same time. There are new people, new noises, new smells and new things to investigate: so be gentle, be affectionate and be as comforting as you can be.

The pup's first day and night in your home can be overwhelming for him. Don't rush the process—go at a pace that keeps the pup calm and content.

PUP'S FIRST NIGHT HOME
You have traveled home with your new charge safely in his crate or on a friend's warm lap. He's been to the vet for a

thorough check-up; he's been weighed, his papers examined; perhaps he's even been vaccinated and wormed as well. He's met the family and licked the whole family, including the excited children and the less-than-happy cat. He's explored his area, his new bed, the garden and anywhere else he's been permitted. He's eaten his first meal at home and relieved himself in the proper place. He's heard lots of new sounds, smelled new friends and seen more of the outside world than ever before.

That was just the first day! He's worn out and is ready for bed...or so you think!

It's puppy's first night and you are ready to say "Good night"—

keep in mind that this is puppy's first night ever to be sleeping alone. His dam and littermates are no longer at paw's length and he's a bit scared, cold and lonely. Be reassuring to your new family member, but this is not the time to spoil him and give in to his inevitable whining.

Puppies whine. They whine to let others know where they are and hopefully to get company out of it. Place your pup in his new bed or crate in his room and close the door. Mercifully, he may fall asleep without a peep. When the inevitable occurs, ignore the whining: he is fine. Be strong and keep his interest in mind. Do not allow yourself to feel guilty and visit the pup. He will fall asleep eventually.

Many breeders recommend placing a piece of bedding from his former home in his new bed so that he recognizes the scent of his littermates. Others still advise placing a hot water bottle in his bed for warmth. This latter may be a good idea provided the pup doesn't attempt to suckle—he'll get good and wet and may not fall asleep so fast.

Puppy's first night can be somewhat stressful for the pup and his new family. Remember that you are setting the tone of nighttime at your house. Unless you want to play with your pup every night at 10 p.m., midnight and 2 a.m., don't initiate the

STRESS-FREE
Some experts in canine health advise that stress during a dog's early years of development can compromise and weaken his immune system, and may trigger the potential for a shortened life. They emphasize the need for happy and stress-free growing-up years.

habit. Your family will thank you, and eventually so will your pup!

PREVENTING PUPPY PROBLEMS

SOCIALIZATION

Now that you have done all of the preparatory work and have helped your pup get accustomed to his new home and family, it is about time for you to have some fun! Socializing your Brittany pup gives you the opportunity to show off your new friend, and your pup gets to reap the benefits of being

Pups will be pups! Harmless rough-housing among littermates is how puppies learn the rules of the canine pack.

IN DUE TIME

It will take at least two weeks for your puppy to become accustomed to his new surroundings. Give him lots of love, attention, handling, frequent opportunities to relieve himself, a diet he likes to eat and a place he can call his own.

the new things he will encounter. Your pup's socialization began with the breeder but now it is your responsibility to continue it. The socialization he receives up until the age of 12 weeks is the most critical, as this is the time when he forms his impressions of the outside world. Be especially careful during the eight-to-ten-week period, also known as the fear period. The interaction he receives during this time should be gentle and reassuring. Lack of socialization can manifest itself in fear and aggression as the dog grows up. He needs lots of human contact, affection,

Your Brittany will fast grow into an active, energetic adolescent dog who needs attention and training on a daily basis.

an adorable furry creature that people will want to pet and, in general, think is absolutely precious!

Besides getting to know his new family, your puppy should be exposed to other people, animals and situations, but of course he must not come into close contact with dogs you don't know well until his course of injections is fully complete. This will help him become well adjusted as he grows up and less prone to being timid or fearful of

handling and exposure to other animals.

Once your pup has received his necessary vaccinations, feel free to take him out and about (on his lead, of course). Walk him around the neighborhood, take him on your daily errands, let people pet him, let him meet other dogs and pets. Puppies do not have to try to make friends; there will be no shortage of people who will want to introduce themselves. Just make sure that you carefully supervise each meeting. If the neighborhood children want to say hello, for example, that is great— children and pups most often make great companions. Sometimes an excited child can unintentionally handle a pup too roughly, or an overzealous pup can playfully nip a little too hard. You want to make socialization experiences positive ones. What a pup learns during this very formative stage will affect his attitude toward future encounters. You want your dog to be comfortable around everyone. A pup that has a bad experience with a child may grow up to be a dog that is shy around or aggressive toward children.

Consistency in Training

Dogs, being pack animals, naturally need a leader, or else they try to establish dominance

PROPER SOCIALIZATION
The socialization period for puppies is from age 8 to 16 weeks. This is the time when puppies need to leave their birth family and take up residence with their new owners, where they will meet many new people, other pets, etc. Failure to be adequately socialized can cause the dog to grow up fearing others and being shy and unfriendly due to a lack of self-confidence.

in their packs. When you welcome a dog into your family, the choice of who becomes the leader and who becomes the "pack" is entirely up to you! Your pup's intuitive quest for dominance, coupled with the fact that it is nearly impossible to look at an adorable Brittany pup with his "puppy-dog" eyes and not cave in, give the pup

MANNERS MATTER

During the socialization process, a puppy should meet people, experience different environments and definitely be exposed to other canines. Through playing and interacting with other dogs, your puppy will learn lessons, ranging from controlling the pressure of his jaws by biting his littermates to the inner-workings of the canine pack that he will apply to his human relationships for the rest of his life. That is why removing a puppy from the litter too early (before eight weeks) can be detrimental to the pup's development.

members do the same. It will only confuse the pup when Mother tells him to get off the sofa when he is used to sitting up there with Father to watch the nightly news. Avoid discrepancies by having all members of the household decide on the rules before the pup even comes home…and be consistent in enforcing them! Early training shapes the dog's personality, so you cannot be unclear in what you expect.

COMMON PUPPY PROBLEMS

The best way to prevent puppy problems is to be proactive in stopping an undesirable behavior as soon as it starts. The old saying "You can't teach an old dog new tricks" does not necessarily hold true, but it is true that it is much

almost an unfair advantage in getting the upper hand! A pup will definitely test the waters to see what he can and cannot do. Do not give in to those pleading eyes—stand your ground when it comes to disciplining the pup and make sure that all family

HOME WITH THE MANGE

Many young dogs suffer from demodectic mange, sometimes called red mange. While all breeds of dog have suffered from demodectic mange, short-coated breeds are at a greater risk. The mange manifests itself as localized infections on the face, muzzle, neck and limbs. The symptoms include hair loss and red, scaly skin. Vets routinely treat demodectic mange so that secondary infections are avoided. Many breeders remove known carriers from their programs.

easier to discourage bad behavior in a young developing pup than to wait until the pup's bad behavior becomes the adult dog's bad habit. There are some problems that are especially prevalent in puppies as they develop.

NIPPING

As puppies start to teethe, they feel the need to sink their teeth into anything available... unfortunately that includes your fingers, arms, hair and toes. You may find this behavior cute for the first five seconds...until you feel just how sharp those puppy teeth are. This is something you want to discourage immediately and consistently with a firm "No!" (or whatever number of firm "No's" it takes for him to understand that you mean business). Then replace your finger with an appropriate chew toy. While this behavior is

Brittanys can be addictive! It's true that all dogs are pack animals, and these owners have chosen to share their home with a veritable "pack" of Brittanys.

TRAINING TIP

Training your puppy takes much patience and can be frustrating at times, but you should see results from your efforts. If you have a puppy that seems untrainable, take him to a trainer or behaviorist. The dog may have a personality problem that requires the help of a professional, or perhaps you need help in learning how to train your dog.

merely annoying when the dog is young, it can become dangerous as your Brittany's adult teeth grow in and his jaws develop, and he continues to think it is okay to gnaw on human appendages. Your Brittany does not mean any harm with a friendly nip, but he also does not know his own strength.

CRYING/WHINING

Your pup will often cry, whine, whimper, howl or make some type of commotion when he is left alone. This is basically his way of calling out for attention to make sure that you know he is there and that you have not forgotten about him. He feels insecure when he is left alone, when you are out of the house and he is in his crate or when you are in another part of the house and he cannot see you. The noise he is making is an expression of the anxiety he feels at being alone, so he needs to be taught that being alone is okay. You are not actually training the dog to stop making noise, you are training him to feel comfortable when he is alone and thus removing the need for him to make the noise. This is where the crate with cozy bedding and a toy comes in handy. You want to know that he is safe when you are not there to supervise, and you know that he will be safe in his crate rather than roaming freely about the house. In order for the

CHEWING TIPS

Chewing goes hand in hand with nipping in the sense that a teething puppy is always looking for a way to soothe his aching gums. In this case, instead of chewing on you, he may have taken a liking to your favorite shoe or something else that he should not be chewing. Again, realize that this is a normal canine behavior that does not need to be discouraged, only redirected. Your pup just needs to be taught what is acceptable to chew on and what is off-limits. Consistently tell him "No!" when you catch him chewing on something forbidden and give him a chew toy.

Conversely, praise him when you catch him chewing on something appropriate. In this way, you are discouraging the inappropriate behavior and reinforcing the desired behavior. The puppy's chewing should stop after his adult teeth have come in, but an adult dog continues to chew for various reasons—perhaps because he is bored, needs to relieve tension or just likes to chew. That is why it is important to redirect his chewing when he is still young.

pup to stay in his crate without making a fuss, he needs to be comfortable in his crate. On that note, it is extremely important that the crate is never used as a form of punishment, or the pup will have a negative association with the crate.

Accustom the pup to the crate in short, gradually increasing time intervals in which you put him in the crate, maybe with a treat, and stay in the room with him. If he cries or makes a fuss, do not go to him, but stay in his sight. Gradually he will realize that staying in his crate is okay without your help, and it will not be so traumatic for him when you are not around. You may want to leave the radio on softly when you leave the house; the sound of human voices may be comforting to him.

EVERYDAY CARE OF YOUR

BRITTANY

The growing Brittany requires a balanced diet and regular exercise to maintain his ideal condition.

Most commercial foods manufactured for dogs meet nutrition standards and list the ingredients contained in the food on every package and can. The ingredients are listed in descending order with the main ingredient listed first.

STORING DOG FOOD
You must store your dry dog food carefully. Open packages of dog food quickly lose their vitamin value, usually within 90 days of being opened. Mold spores and vermin could also contaminate the food.

FEEDING YOUR BRITTANY
By the time your Brittany puppy is 12 months old, you can reduce feedings to one or two a day—morning and night. Feed meals at the same time every day and make sure what you feed is nutritionally complete.

Refined sugars are not a part of the canine natural food acquisition and canine teeth are not genetically disposed to handling these sugars. Do not feed your Brittany sugar products and avoid products that contain sugar to any high degree.

Fresh water and a properly prepared, balanced diet containing the essential nutrients in correct proportions are all a healthy Brittany needs to be offered. Dog foods come tinned, dried, semi-moist, "scientifically fortified" and "all-natural." A visit to your local grocery or pet store will reveal how vast an array from which you will be able to select.

All dogs, whether large or small, are carnivorous (meat-eating) animals. Animal protein and fats are essential to the well-being of your Brittany. However, a diet too high in proteins can lead to problems as well. Not all dry foods contain the necessary amount of protein a Brittany requires to keep it in top condition. It is best to discuss this with the breeder from whom you buy your dog or with your veterinarian.

Over-feeding is very harmful to the Brittany. It puts stress on the kidneys and heart. It also can make a Brittany very lazy and disinterested in the exercise necessary to keep the breed in shape.

The domesticated dog's diet must include protein, carbohy-

FOOD PREFERENCE

Selecting the best dry dog food is difficult. There is no majority consensus among veterinary scientists as to the value of nutrient analysis (protein, fat, fiber, moisture, ash, cholesterol, minerals, etc.). All agree that feeding trials are what matter most, but you also have to consider the individual dog. The dog's weight, age and activity level, and what pleases his taste, all must be considered. It is probably best to take the advice of your veterinarian. Every dog has individual dietary requirements, and should be fed accordingly.

If your dog is fed a good dry food, he does not require supplements of meat or vegetables. Dogs do appreciate a little variety in their diets, so you may choose to stay with the same brand but vary the flavor. Alternatively, you may wish to add a little flavored stock to give a difference to the taste.

DO DOGS HAVE TASTE BUDS?

Watching a dog "wolf" or gobble his food, seemingly without chewing, leads an owner to wonder whether his dog can taste anything. Yes, dogs have taste buds, with sensory perception of sweet, salty and sour. Puppies are born with fully mature taste buds.

ents your Brittany needs. It is therefore unnecessary to add vitamin supplements to these diets in other than special circumstances prescribed by your vet.

These special periods in a Brittany's life can include the time of rapid growth the breed experiences in puppyhood, the female's pregnancy and the time during which she is nursing her puppies. A Brittany that has a heavy schedule in the field may benefit from vitamin supplementation as well but, here again, the amounts and frequency should be monitored.

Over-supplementation and forced growth are now looked upon by some breeders as major contributors to many skeletal abnormalities found in the pure-bred dogs of the day. Some claim these problems and a wide variety of chronic skin conditions are entirely hereditary but many others feel they can be exacerbated by diet and over-use of mineral and vitamin supplements in puppies.

WATER

Just as your dog needs proper nutrition from his food, water is an essential "nutrient" as well. Water keeps the dog's body properly hydrated and promotes normal function of the body's systems. During house-training, it is necessary to keep an eye on

drates, fats, roughage and small amounts of essential minerals and vitamins. Many breeders strongly recommend adding small amounts of cooked vegetables to a Brittany's diet. This provides the necessary carbohydrates, minerals and nutrients present only in vegetables.

Commercially prepared foods contain all the necessary nutri-

how much water your Brittany is drinking, but once he is reliably trained he should have access to clean fresh water at all times, especially if you feed dry food. Make certain that the dog's water bowl is clean, and change the water often.

EXERCISE

Exercise is a bottom-line fact of a Brittany's life. The Brittany was bred to work day in and day out in the field, and that ability and need remain with the breed to this day. A well-exercised Brittany can live happily in an apartment in a big city, but understand the operative word here is "well-exercised." The bored, inactive Brittany would be miserable and destructive in any environment, no less a confining one.

Mature Brittanys are capable and delighted jogging companions. It is important, however, to use good judgment in any exercise program. Begin slowly and increase the distance to be covered very gradually over an extended period of time. Use special precautions in hot weather. High temperatures and forced exercise are a dangerous combination.

Needless to say, puppies should never be forced to exercise. Normally, they are little dynamos of energy and keep themselves busy all day long, interspersed with frequent naps.

DRINK, DRANK, DRUNK— MAKE IT A DOUBLE

In both humans and dogs, as well as other living organisms, water forms the major part of nearly every body tissue. Naturally, we take water for granted, but without it, life as we know it would cease.

For dogs, water is needed to keep their bodies functioning biochemically. Additionally, water is needed to replace the water lost while panting. Unlike humans, who are able to sweat to dissipate heat, dogs must pant to cool down, thereby losing the vital water that their bodies need to regulate their body temperatures. Humans lose electrolyte-containing products and other body-fluid components through sweating; dogs do not lose anything except water.

Water is essential always, but especially so when the weather is hot or humid or when your dog is exercising or working vigorously.

A Worthy Investment

Veterinary studies have proven that a balanced high-quality diet pays off in your dog's coat quality, behavior and activity level. Invest in premium brands for the maximum payoff with your dog.

The best exercise for a Brittany is that which he acquires in the pursuit of the many organized activities for which the breed is particularly well suited. Hunting, agility, flyball and obedience activities exercise the Brittany's mind and body. There is no better way to ensure your Brittany of a happy, healthy existence.

GROOMING

The Brittany is a natural breed that requires hardly any clipping or trimming. Anything that has to be done can be done with a pair of straight shears, thinning shears and a brush. Regular thorough brushing and a bath when necessary are important parts of keeping your dog a clean, healthy and pleasant companion.

You can dry-bathe your Brittany by sprinkling a little baby powder in the coat, working it well in and then brushing it out. This, of course, also helps to make the dog smell very good.

Over-bathing can lead to dry-skin problems. Dry skin creates a need to scratch and this can lead to severe scratching and "hot spots," moist sore areas in which the coat is entirely scratched away.

The easiest way to groom a Brittany is by placing it on a

There are so many ways to exercise your energetic Brittany. His versatile nature makes him easily trainable to a number of activities, and you'll find that he's a willing participant!

grooming table. Make sure the table is of a height at which you can work comfortably either sitting or standing. Adjustable-height grooming tables are available at most pet outlets.

It is best to use a grooming table that has an "arm" and a "noose." The noose slips around the dog's neck when he is standing and keeps the dog from fidgeting about or jumping down when he has decided he has had enough grooming.

Invest in a good natural bristle brush that has some nylon

Although a natural breed that requires no special grooming, show Brittanys are touched up before appearing in the ring so that their coats look healthy and neat.

EXERCISE ALERT!
You should be careful where you exercise your dog. Many areas have been sprayed with chemicals that are highly toxic to both dogs and humans. Never allow your dog to eat grass or drink from puddles on either public or private grounds, as the run-off water may contain chemicals from sprays and herbicides.

bristles inserted in it. You will also need a steel comb to remove any debris that collects in the longer furnishings. A comb that has teeth divided between fine and coarse is ideal.

When brushing, proceed vigorously from behind the head to the tail. Do this all over the body and be especially careful to attend to the hard-to-reach areas between the legs, behind the ears and under the body. A good Brittany coat seldom mats or tangles. However, mats can occur when the dog is casting his puppy coat or if an adult catches burrs or sticky substances in his longer furnishings.

Should you encounter a mat that does not brush out easily, use your fingers and the steel comb to separate the hairs as much as possible. Do not cut or pull out the matted hair. Apply baby powder or one of the especially prepared grooming powders directly to the mat and brush completely from the skin out.

The coat of a neutered Brittany, male or female, will be softer and longer than that of unaltered dogs. It is helpful to strip the coat of a neutered Brittany two or three time a year to keep the coat harsher and in a more natural state. A stripping knife is used for this purpose and the breeder from which the Brittany is purchased can

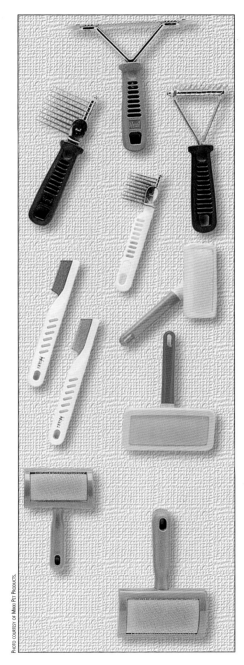

PHOTO COURTESY OF MIKKI PET PRODUCTS.

Your local pet shop will have many types of combs and brushes from which you can select suitable tools for grooming your Brittany.

Accustom the young puppy to the feel of a comb. This will make adult grooming sessions easier to manage.

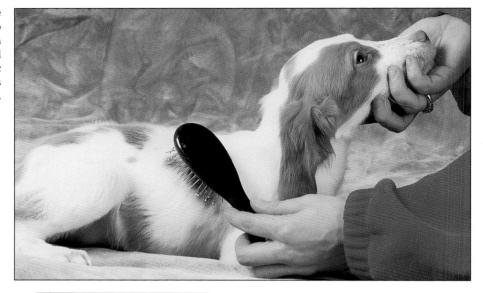

GROOMING EQUIPMENT

Always purchase the best quality grooming equipment so that your tools will last for many years to come. Here are some basics:

- Grooming table
- Natural and nylon bristle brush
- Metal comb
- Thinning shears
- Straight shears
- Stripping knife (optional)
- Electric clipper (optional)
- Ear powder
- Cotton balls
- Nail clippers or drummel
- Dental-care products
- Rubber mat
- Dog shampoo
- Spray hose attachment
- Towels
- Blow dryer

instruct most any owner how to accomplish the procedure.

NAIL TRIMMING

The grooming session is a good time to accustom your Brittany to having his nails trimmed and having his feet inspected. Always inspect your dog's feet for cracked pads. Check between the toes for splinters and thorns, paying particular attention to any swollen or tender areas.

Attend to your dog's nails at least every three to four weeks. Long nails spread and weaken the foot. The nails of a Brittany that isn't exercising outdoors on rough terrain will grow long very quickly.

Each nail has a blood vessel running through the center

called the "quick." The quick grows close to the end of the nail and contains very sensitive nerve endings. If the nail is allowed to grow too long, it will be more difficult to cut it back to a proper length without cutting into the quick. This causes severe pain to the dog and can also result in a great deal of bleeding that can be very difficult to stop.

Nails can be trimmed with canine nail clippers or an electric nail grinder called a drummel. Use the "fine" grinding disc on the drummel because this allows you to trim back the nail a little bit at a time, practically eliminating causing any bleeding to occur.

Always proceed with caution and remove only a small portion

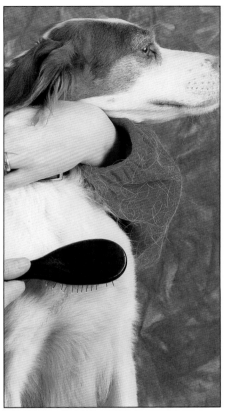

Combing the Brittany will remove any debris from the coat and keep it looking shiny and clean.

of the nail at a time. Should the quick be nipped in the trimming process, there are any number of blood-clotting products available at pet shops that will almost immediately stem the flow of blood. It is wise to have one of these products on hand in case your dog breaks a nail in some way.

HUNTING OR UTILITY CLIP

Trimming a Brittany for hunting ahead of time will save all kinds

PEDICURE TIP

A dog that spends a lot of time outside on a hard surface, such as cement or pavement, will have his nails naturally worn down and may not need to have them trimmed as often, except maybe in the colder months when he is not outside as much. Regardless, it is best to get your dog accustomed to the nail-trimming procedure at an early age so that he is used to it. Some dogs are especially sensitive about having their feet touched, but if a dog has experienced it since puppyhood, it should not bother him.

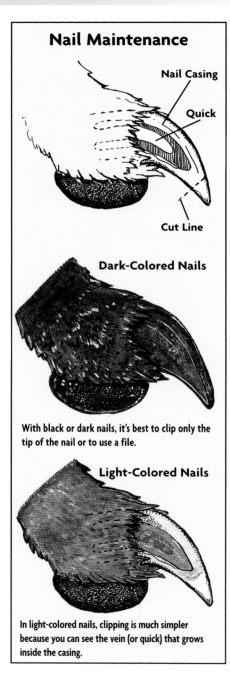

Nail Maintenance

Nail Casing

Quick

Cut Line

Dark-Colored Nails

With black or dark nails, it's best to clip only the tip of the nail or to use a file.

Light-Colored Nails

In light-colored nails, clipping is much simpler because you can see the vein (or quick) that grows inside the casing.

of work when the hunt is over. Also, the terrain you and your dog cover when the two of you go hiking will determine how much hair will be appropriate. This method can be modified to accommodate the situation.

To begin, lift the ear and take out all the excess hair on the upper cheek and under the ear. This is one of the worst places for picking up and holding burrs, stickers and other debris. You can use thinning shears or an electric clipper with a #10 blade to do this.

Hold the ear out from the head and cut off all hair that is longer than the ear leather. Use straight shears for this. If the hair on the top of the ear becomes too thick, it can be stripped using a stripping knife or thinning shears.

The hair in the armpits, where the legs join the body, should also be cut away to protect against collecting burrs. Do not shave the underline of the Brittany as removing all hair exposes the belly to become scratched and sore. The hair in this area should be trimmed to about an inch in length to provide protection.

Feet should be tidied up by removing all excess hair between the toes and trimming any excess around the foot. This helps to keep the foxtails and other field debris from catching between the

SOAP IT UP

The use of human soap products like shampoo, bubble bath and hand soap can be damaging to a dog's coat and skin. Human products are too strong; they remove the protective oils coating the dog's hair and skin that make him water-resistant. Use only shampoo made especially for dogs. You may like to use a medicated shampoo, which will help to keep external parasites at bay.

remove when the coat is wet. Make certain that your dog has a good non-slip mat to stand on. Begin by wetting the dog's coat. A shower or hose attachment is necessary for thoroughly wetting and rinsing the coat. Check the water temperature to make sure that it is neither too hot nor too cold.

Using an adjustable-height grooming table makes the job of grooming a Brittany much easier.

toes as well as making it easy to check when coming out of the field.

Brittanys are inclined to grow a "flag" on their tails. Some owners like this flag, and some do not. Shape the hair neatly using thinning shears, if desired.

BATHING

Dogs do not need to be bathed as often as humans, but regular bathing is essential for healthy skin and a healthy, shiny coat. Again, like most anything, if you accustom your pup to being bathed as a puppy, it will be second nature by the time he grows up. You want your dog to be at ease in the bathtub or else it could end up a wet, soapy, messy ordeal for both of you!

Brush your Brittany thoroughly before wetting his coat. This will get rid of any debris or tangles, which are harder to

Show dogs are bathed before every show. They must be patient while their handlers apply the finishing touches.

Next, apply shampoo to the dog's coat and work it into a good lather. You should purchase a shampoo that is made for dogs. Do not use a product made for human hair. Wash the head last; you do not want shampoo to drip into the dog's eyes while you are washing the rest of his body. Work the shampoo all the way down to the skin. You can use this opportunity to check the skin for any bumps, bites or other abnormalities. Do not neglect any area of the body—get all of the hard-to-reach places.

Once the dog has been thoroughly shampooed, he requires an equally thorough rinsing. Shampoo left in the coat can be irritating to the skin. Protect his eyes from the shampoo by shielding them with your hand and directing the flow of water in the opposite direction. You should also avoid getting water in the

It is safer to clean the dog's ears with a cotton ball than to use a cotton swab, which requires a very gentle touch.

ear canal. Be prepared for your dog to shake out his coat—you might want to stand back, but make sure you have a hold on the dog to keep him from running through the house.

EAR CLEANING
The ears should be kept clean with a cotton ball and ear

powder made especially for dogs. Be on the lookout for any signs of infection or ear-mite infestation. If your Brittany has been shaking his head or scratching at his ears frequently, this usually indicates a problem. If his ears have an unusual odor, this is a sure sign of mite infestation or infection, and a signal to have his ears checked by the veterinarian.

TRAVELING WITH YOUR DOG

CAR TRAVEL
You should accustom your Brittany to riding in a car at an early age. You may or may not take him in the car often, but at the very least he will need to go to the vet and you do not want these trips to be traumatic for the dog or troublesome for you. The safest way for a dog to ride in the car is in his crate. If he uses a crate in the house, you can use the same crate for travel.

Put the pup in the crate and see how he reacts. If he seems uneasy, you can have a passenger hold him on his lap while you drive. Another option is a specially made safety harness for dogs, which straps the dog in much like a seat belt. Do not let the dog roam loose in the vehicle—this is very dangerous! If you should stop short, your dog can be thrown and injured. If the dog starts climbing on you and pestering you while

BATHING BEAUTY
Once you are sure that the dog is thoroughly rinsed, squeeze the excess water out of his coat with your hand and dry him with an heavy towel. You may choose to use a blow dryer on his coat or just let it dry naturally. In cold weather, never allow your dog outside with a wet coat.

There are "dry bath" products on the market, which are sprays and powders intended for spot cleaning, that can be used between regular baths if necessary. They are not substitutes for regular baths, but they are easy to use for touch-ups as they do not require rinsing.

LET THE SUN SHINE

Your dog needs daily sunshine for the same reason people do. Pets kept inside homes with curtains drawn against the sun suffer from "SAD" (Seasonal Affected Disorder) to the same degree as humans. We now know that sunlight must enter the iris and thus progress to the pineal gland to regulate the body's hormonal system. When we live and work in artificial light, both circadian rhythms and hormone balances are disturbed.

AIR TRAVEL

If bringing your dog on a flight, you will have to contact the airline to make special arrangements. It is rather common for dogs to travel by air, so major airlines have policies and procedures for pet travel. The dog will be required to travel in an airline-approved crate; you may be able to use your own or the airline can usually supply one at extra cost. To help the dog be at ease, put one of his favorite toys in the crate with him. Do not feed the dog for several hours before the trip to minimize his need to relieve himself. However, you must certify that the dog has been given food and water within a certain timeframe of check-in.

Make sure your dog is properly identified and that your contact information appears on his ID tags and on his crate. Animals travel in a different area of the plane than human passengers so every rule must be strictly followed so as to prevent

When traveling with your Brittany in a car, always keep the dog safe in his crate or with a special car harness.

you are driving, you will not be able to concentrate on the road. It is an unsafe situation for everyone—human and canine.

For long trips, be prepared to stop to let the dog relieve himself. Take with you whatever you need to clean up after him, including some paper towels and perhaps some old towels for use should he have an accident in the car or suffer from motion sickness.

Your Brittany is indeed valuable cargo—make sure he's properly identified and feeling well before any air travel.

MOTION SICKNESS

*If life is a motorway...*your dog may not want to come along for the ride! Some dogs experience motion sickness in cars that leads to excessive salivation and even vomiting. In most cases, your dog will fare better in the familiar, safe confines of his crate. To desensitize your dog, try going on several short jaunts before trying a long trip. If your dog experiences distress when riding in the vehicle, drive with him only when absolutely necessary, and do not feed him or give him water before you go.

the risk of getting separated from your dog.

BOARDING AND VACATIONS

So you want to take a family vacation—and you want to include *all* members of the family. You would probably make arrangements for accommodations ahead of time anyway, but this is especially important when traveling with a dog. You do not want to make an overnight stop at the only place around for miles and find out that they do not allow dogs. Also, you do not want to reserve a place for your family without confirming that you are traveling with a dog because if it is against their policy you may not have a place to stay.

Alternatively, if you are traveling and choose not to bring

your Brittany, you will have to make arrangements for him while you are away. Some options are to take him to a neighbor's house to stay while

Visit local boarding kennels and select the kennel that best suits your needs. You are advised to research several kennels and select one before you actually require its services.

you are gone, to have a trusted neighbor stop by often or stay at your house or to bring your dog to a reputable boarding kennel. If you choose to board him at a kennel, you should visit in advance to see the facilities provided, how clean they are and where the dogs are kept. Talk to some of the employees and see how they treat the dogs—do they spend time with the dogs, play with them, exercise them, etc.? Also find out the kennel's policy on vaccinations and what they require. This is for all of the dogs' safety, since when dogs are kept together, there is a greater risk of diseases being passed from dog to dog.

TRAVEL TIP

When traveling, never let your dog off-lead in a strange area. Your dog could run away out of fear, decide to chase a passing squirrel or cat or simply want to stretch his legs without restriction—if any of these happen, you might never see your canine friend again.

Your pet Brittany should have his collar and ID tag at all times, even when just hanging around the backyard.

IDENTIFICATION

Your Brittany is your valued companion and friend. That is why you always keep a close eye on him and you have made sure that he cannot escape from the yard or wriggle out of his collar and run away from you. However, accidents can happen and there may come a time when your dog unexpectedly gets separated from you. If this unfortunate event should occur, the first thing on your mind will be finding him. Proper identification, including an ID tag and possibly a microchip, will increase the chances of his being returned to you safely and quickly. Some owners also consider tattooing the dog, though most prefer the convenience of a microchip, which can be inserted at the same time the pet dog is spayed or neutered.

No dog should ever be without his identification tags, which should be securely attached to his everyday collar.

Living with an untrained dog is a lot like owning a piano that you do not know how to play—it is a nice object to look at but it does not do much more than that to bring you pleasure. Now try taking piano lessons and suddenly the piano comes alive and brings forth magical sounds and rhythms that set your heart singing and your body swaying.

The same is true with your Brittany. Any dog is a big responsibility and if not trained sensibly may develop unacceptable behavior that annoys you or could even cause family friction.

To train your Brittany, you may like to enroll in an obedience class. Teach him good manners as you learn how and why he behaves the way he does. Find out how to communicate with your dog and how to recognize and understand his communications with you. Suddenly the dog takes on a new role in your life—he is clever, interesting, well-behaved and fun to be with. He demonstrates his bond of devotion to you daily. In other words, your Brittany does wonders for your ego because he constantly reminds you that you are not only his leader, you are his hero!

Those involved with teaching dog obedience and counseling owners about their dogs' behavior have discovered some interesting

REAP THE REWARDS
If you start with a normal, healthy dog and give him time, patience and some carefully executed lessons, you will reap the rewards of that training for the life of the dog. And what a life it will be! The two of you will find immeasurable pleasure in the companionship you have built together with love, respect and understanding.

facts about dog ownership. For example, training dogs when they are puppies results in the highest rate of success in developing well-mannered and well-adjusted adult dogs. Training an older dog, from six months to six years of age, can produce almost equal results providing that the owner accepts the dog's slower rate of learning capability and is willing to work patiently to help the dog succeed at developing to his fullest potential. Unfortunately, many owners of untrained adult dogs lack the patience factor, so they do not persist until their dogs are successful at learning particular behaviors.

Training a puppy aged 10 to 16 weeks (20 weeks at the most) is like working with a dry sponge in a pool of water. The pup soaks up whatever you show him and constantly looks for more things to do and learn. At this early age, his body is not yet producing hormones, and therein lies the reason for such a high rate of success. Without hormones, he is focused on his owners and not particularly interested in investigating other places, dogs, people, etc. You are his leader: his provider of food, water, shelter and security. He latches onto you and wants to stay close. He will usually follow you from room to room, will not let you out of his sight when you are outdoors with him and will

PARENTAL GUIDANCE
Training a dog is a life experience. Many parents admit that much of what they know about raising children they learned from caring for their dogs. Dogs respond to love, fairness and guidance, just as children do. Become a good dog owner and you may become an even better parent.

At the tender age of ten weeks, the Brittany pup is ready to soak up whatever you choose to teach him.

respond in like manner to the people and animals you encounter. If you greet a friend warmly, he will be happy to greet the person as well. If, however, you are hesitant, even anxious, about the approach of a stranger, he will respond accordingly.

Once the puppy begins to produce hormones, his natural curiosity emerges and he begins to investigate the world around him. It is at this time when you may notice that the untrained

MEALTIME

Mealtime should be a peaceful time for your puppy. Do not put his food and water bowls in a high-traffic area in the house. For example, give him his own little corner of the kitchen where he can eat undisturbed and where he will not be underfoot. Do not allow small children or other family members to disturb the pup when he is eating.

dog begins to wander away from you and even ignore your commands to stay close. When this behavior becomes a problem, the owner has two choices: get rid of the dog or train him. It is strongly urged that you choose the latter option.

There are usually classes within a reasonable distance from the owner's home, but you can also do a lot to train your dog yourself. Sometimes there are classes available but the tuition is too costly. Whatever the circumstances, the solution to training your Brittany without formal classes lies within the pages of this book. This chapter is devoted to helping you train your Brittany at home. If the recommended procedures are followed faithfully, you may expect positive results that will prove rewarding both to you and your dog.

Whether your new charge is a puppy or a mature adult, the methods of teaching and the techniques we use in training basic behaviors are the same. After all, no dog, whether puppy or adult, likes harsh or inhumane methods. All creatures, however, respond favorably to gentle motivational methods and sincere praise and encouragement. Now let us get started.

HOUSE-TRAINING

You can train a puppy to relieve himself wherever you choose, but this must be somewhere suitable. You should bear in mind from the outset that when your puppy is old enough to go out in public places, any canine droppings must be removed at once. You will always have to carry with you a small plastic bag or "poop-scoop."

Outdoor training includes such surfaces as grass, soil and cement. Indoor training usually means training your dog to newspaper. When deciding on the surface and location that you will want your Brittany to use, be sure it is going to be perma-

nent. Training your dog to grass and then changing your mind two months later is extremely difficult for both dog and owner.

Next, choose the command you will use each and every time you want your puppy to void.

HOW MANY TIMES A DAY?

AGE	RELIEF TRIPS
To 14 weeks	10
14–22 weeks	8
22–32 weeks	6
Adulthood	4
(dog stops growing)	

These are estimates, of course, but they are a guide to the *minimum* number of opportunities a dog should have each day to relieve himself.

HONOR AND OBEY

Dogs are the most honorable animals in existence. They consider another species (humans) as their own. They interface with you. You are their leader. Puppies perceive children to be on their level; their actions around small children are different from their behavior around their adult masters.

"Hurry up" and "Go potty" are examples of commands commonly used by dog owners. Get in the habit of giving the puppy your chosen relief command before you take him out. That way, when he becomes an adult, you will be able to determine if he wants to go out when you ask him. A confirmation will be signs of interest, such as wagging his tail, watching you intently, going to the door, etc.

PUPPY'S NEEDS

Your puppy needs to relieve himself after play periods, after each meal, after he has been sleeping and at any time he indicates that he is looking for a place to urinate or defecate. The urinary and intestinal tract muscles of very young puppies are not fully developed. Therefore, like human babies, puppies need to relieve themselves frequently.

Take your puppy out often— every hour for an eight-week-old, for example, and always immediately after sleeping and eating. The older the puppy, the less often he will need to relieve himself. Finally, as a mature healthy adult, he will require only three to five relief trips per day.

HOUSING

Since the types of housing and control you provide for your

CANINE DEVELOPMENT SCHEDULE

It is important to understand how and at what age a puppy develops into adulthood. If you are a puppy owner, consult the following Canine Development Schedule to determine the stage of development your puppy is currently experiencing. This knowledge will help you as you work with the puppy in the weeks and months ahead.

Period	Age	Characteristics
First to Third	Birth to Seven Weeks	Puppy needs food, sleep and warmth, and responds to simple and gentle touching. Needs mother for security and disciplining. Needs littermates for learning and interacting with other dogs. Pup learns to function within a pack and learns pack order of dominance. Begin socializing pup with adults and children for short periods. Pup begins to become aware of his environment.
Fourth	Eight to Twelve Weeks	Brain is fully developed. Pup needs socializing with outside world. Remove from mother and littermates. Needs to change from canine pack to human pack. Human dominance necessary. Fear period occurs between 8 and 12 weeks. Avoid fright and pain.
Fifth	Thirteen to Sixteen Weeks	Training and formal obedience should begin. Less association with other dogs, more with people, places, situations. Period will pass easily if you remember this is pup's change-to-adolescence time. Be firm and fair. Flight instinct prominent. Permissiveness and over-disciplining can do permanent damage. Praise for good behavior.
Juvenile	Four to Eight Months	Another fear period about 7 to 8 months of age. It passes quickly, but be cautious of fright and pain. Sexual maturity reached. Dominant traits established. Dog should understand sit, down, come and stay by now.

NOTE: THESE ARE APPROXIMATE TIME FRAMES. ALLOW FOR INDIVIDUAL DIFFERENCES IN PUPPIES.

positive reinforcers that he is now a member of your pack. Usually a family room, the kitchen or a nearby adjoining breakfast area is ideal for providing safety and security for both puppy and owner.

Within that room there should be a smaller area that the puppy can call his own. An alcove, a wire or fiberglass dog crate or a gated corner from which he can view the activities of his new family will be fine. The size of the area or crate is the key factor here. The area must be large enough for the puppy to lie down and stretch out as well as stand up without rubbing his head on the top, yet

Male dogs are notoriously more difficult to housebreak, partly due to their instinct to mark their territory with small amounts of urine.

puppy have a direct relationship on the success of house-training, we consider the various aspects of both before we begin training. Taking a new puppy home and turning him loose in your house can be compared to turning a child loose in a sports arena and telling the child that the place is all his! The sheer enormity of the place would be too much for him to handle.

Instead, offer the puppy clearly defined areas where he can play, sleep, eat and live. A room of the house where the family gathers is the most obvious choice. Puppies are social animals and need to feel a part of the pack right from the start. Hearing your voice, watching you while you are doing things and smelling you nearby are all

---

PRACTICE MAKES PERFECT!

- Have training lessons with your dog every day in several short segments—three to five times a day for a few minutes at a time is ideal.
- Do not have long practice sessions. The dog will become easily bored.
- Never practice when you are tired, ill, worried or in an otherwise negative mood. This will transmit to the dog and may have an adverse effect on his performance.

Think fun, short and above all *positive!* End each session on a high note, rather than a failed exercise, and make sure to give a lot of praise. Enjoy the training and help your dog enjoy it, too.

small enough so that he cannot relieve himself at one end and sleep at the other without coming into contact with his droppings until fully trained to relieve himself outside. The designated area should contain clean bedding and a toy. Water must always be available, in a non-spill container.

Dogs are, by nature, clean animals and will not remain close to their relief areas unless forced to do so. In those cases, they then become dirty dogs and usually remain that way for life.

CONTROL

By *control*, we mean helping the puppy to create a lifestyle pattern that will be compatible to that of his human pack (*you!*). Just as we guide little children to learn our way of life, we must show the puppy when it is time to play, eat, sleep, exercise and even entertain himself.

Your puppy should always sleep in his crate. He should also learn that, during times of household confusion and excessive human activity such as at breakfast when family members are preparing for the day, he can play by himself in relative safety and comfort in his designated area. Each time you leave the puppy alone, he should understand exactly where he is to stay. Puppies are chewers. They cannot tell the difference

FEAR AGGRESSION

Pups who are subjected to physical abuse during training commonly end up with behavioral problems as adults. One common result of abuse is fear aggression, in which a dog will lash out, bare his teeth, snarl and finally bite someone by whom he feels threatened. For example, your daughter may be playing with the dog one afternoon. As they play hide-and-seek, she backs the dog into a corner and, as she attempts to tease him playfully, he bites her hand. Examine the cause of this behavior. Did your daughter ever hit the dog? Did someone who resembles your daughter hit or scream at the dog?

Fortunately, fear aggression is relatively easy to correct. Have your daughter engage in only positive activities with the dog, such as feeding, petting and walking. She should not give any corrections or negative feedback. If the dog still growls or cowers away from her, allow someone else to accompany them. After approximately one week, the dog should feel that he can rely on her for many positive things, and he will also be prevented from reacting fearfully towards anyone who might resemble her.

pable of making the association of the discipline with his naughty deed.)

Other times of excitement, such as family parties, visits, etc., can be fun for the puppy providing he can view the activities from the security of his designated area. He is not underfoot and he is not being fed all sorts of tidbits that will probably cause him stomach distress, yet he still feels a part of the fun.

SCHEDULE

A puppy should be taken to his relief area each time he is released from his designated area, after meals, after play sessions and when he first awakens in the morning (at age eight weeks, this can mean 5 a.m.!). The puppy will indicate that he's

Breeders know that all dogs learn by watching. Young pups can learn good behavior (and bad habits) by observing how adults behave.

between lamp cords, television wires, shoes, table legs, etc. Chewing into a television wire, for example, can be fatal to the puppy while a shorted wire can start a fire in the house.

If the puppy chews on the arm of the chair when he is alone, you will probably discipline him angrily when you get home. Thus, he makes the association that your coming home means he is going to be punished. (He will not remember chewing the chair and is inca-

THE CLEAN LIFE

By providing sleeping and resting quarters that fit the dog, and offering frequent opportunities to relieve himself outside his quarters, the puppy quickly learns that the outdoors (or the newspaper if you are training him to paper) is the place to go when he needs to urinate or defecate. It also reinforces his innate desire to keep his sleeping quarters clean. This, in turn, helps develop the muscle control that will eventually produce a dog with clean living habits.

ready "to go" by circling or sniffing busily—do not misinterpret these signs. For a puppy less than ten weeks of age, a routine of taking him out every hour is necessary. As the puppy grows, he will be able to wait for longer periods of time.

Keep trips to his relief area short. Stay no more than five or six minutes and then return to the house. If he goes during that time, praise him lavishly and take him indoors immediately. If he does not, but he has an accident when you go back indoors, pick him up immediately, say "No! No!" and return to his relief area. Wait a few minutes, then return to the house again. Never

THE SUCCESS METHOD

6 Steps to Successful Crate Training

1 Tell the puppy "Crate time!" and place him in the crate with a small treat (a piece of cheese or half of a biscuit). Let him stay in the crate for five minutes while you are in the same room. Then release him and praise lavishly. Never release him when he is fussing. Wait until he is quiet before you let him out.

2 Repeat Step 1 several times a day.

3 The next day, place the puppy in the crate as before. Let him stay there for ten minutes. Do this several times.

4 Continue building time in five-minute increments until the puppy stays in his crate for 30 minutes with you in the room. Always take him to his relief area after prolonged periods in his crate.

5 Now go back to Step 1 and let the puppy stay in his crate for five minutes, this time while you are out of the room.

6 Once again, build crate time in five-minute increments with you out of the room. When the puppy will stay willingly in his crate (he may even fall asleep!) for 30 minutes with you out of the room, he will be ready to stay in it for several hours at a time.

THE SUCCESS METHOD

Success that comes by luck is usually short-lived. Success that comes by well-thought-out proven methods is often more easily achieved and permanent. This is the Success Method. It is designed to give you, the puppy owner, a simple yet proven way to help your puppy develop clean living habits and a feeling of security in his new environment.

hit a puppy or put his face in urine or excrement when he has had an accident!

Once indoors, put the puppy in his crate until you have had time to clean up his accident. Then release him to the family area and watch him more closely than before. Chances are, his accident was a result of your not picking up his signal or waiting too long before offering him the opportunity to relieve himself. Never hold a grudge against the puppy for accidents.

Let the puppy learn that going outdoors means it is time to relieve himself, not play. Once trained, he will be able to play indoors and out and still differentiate between the times for play versus the times for relief. Help him develop regular hours for naps, being alone, playing by himself and just resting, all in his crate. Encourage him to entertain himself while you are busy with your activities. Let him learn that having you near is comforting, but it is not your main purpose in life to provide him with undivided attention.

Each time you put a puppy in his own area, use the same command, whatever suits best. Soon he will run to his crate or special area when he hears you say those words. Crate training provides safety for you, the puppy and the home. It also provides the puppy with a feeling of security, and that helps the puppy achieve self-confidence and clean habits.

Remember that one of the primary ingredients in house-training your puppy is control. Regardless of your lifestyle, there will always be occasions when you will need to have a place where your dog can stay and be happy and safe. Crate training is the answer for now and in the future.

The crate provides your Brittany with a den, a place of refuge, a place to call his own in the home. Once accustomed to the crate, he will go there willingly and will make every effort to keep it clean.

In conclusion, a few key elements are really all you need for a successful house-training method—consistency, frequency, praise, control and supervision. By following these procedures with a normal, healthy puppy, you and the puppy will soon be past the stage of accidents and ready to move on to a clean and rewarding life together.

ROLES OF DISCIPLINE, REWARD AND PUNISHMENT

Discipline, training one to act in accordance with rules, brings order to life. It is as simple as that. Without discipline, particularly in a group society, chaos reigns supreme and the group will eventually perish. Humans and canines are social animals and need some form of discipline in order to function effectively. They must procure food, reproduce to keep the species going and protect their home base and their young.

If there were no discipline in the lives of social animals, they would eventually die from starvation and/or predation by other stronger animals. In the case of domestic canines, dogs need discipline in their lives in order to understand how their pack (you and other family members) functions and how they must act in order to survive.

A large humane society in a highly populated area recently surveyed dog owners regarding their satisfaction with their relationships with their dogs. People who had trained their dogs were 75% more satisfied with their pets than those who had never trained their dogs.

Dr. Edward Thorndike, a noted psychologist, established *Thorndike's Theory of Learning*, which states that a behavior that results in a pleasant event tends to be repeated. Likewise, a behavior that results in an unpleasant event tends not to be repeated. It is this theory on which training methods are based today. For example, if you manipulate a dog to perform a specific behavior and reward him for doing it, he is likely to do it again because he enjoyed the end result.

Occasionally, punishment, a penalty inflicted for an offense, is necessary. The best type of punishment often comes from an outside source. For example, a child is told not to touch the stove because he may get burned.

THINK BEFORE YOU BARK
Dogs are sensitive to their masters' moods and emotions. Use your voice wisely when communicating with your dog. Never raise your voice at your dog unless you are trying to correct him. "Barking" at your dog can become as meaningless as "dogspeak" is to you.

He disobeys and touches the stove. In doing so, he receives a burn. From that time on, he respects the heat of the stove and avoids contact with it. Therefore, a behavior that results in an unpleasant event tends not to be repeated.

A good example of a dog learning the hard way is the dog who chases the house cat. He is told many times to leave the cat alone, yet he persists in teasing the cat. Then, one day he begins chasing the cat but the cat turns and swipes a claw across the dog's face, leaving him with a painful gash on his nose. The final result is that the dog stops chasing the cat.

TRAINING EQUIPMENT

COLLAR AND LEAD

For a Brittany, the collar and lead that you use for training must be one with which you are easily able to work, not too heavy for the dog and perfectly safe.

> ## THE GOLDEN RULE
> The golden rule of dog training is simple. For each "question" (command), there is only one correct answer (reaction). One command = one reaction. Keep practicing the command until the dog reacts correctly without hesitating. Be repetitive but not monotonous. Dogs get bored just as people do!

A reward in the form of a tasty tidbit can yield immediate results.

TREATS

Have a bag of treats on hand. Something nutritious and easy to swallow works best. Use a soft treat, a chunk of cheese or a piece of cooked chicken rather than a dry biscuit. By the time the dog has finished chewing a dry treat, he will forget why he is being rewarded in the first place! Using food rewards, incidentally, will not teach a dog to beg at the table—the only way to teach a dog to beg at the table is to give him food from the table. In training, rewarding the dog with a food treat will help him associate praise and the treats with learning new behaviors that obviously please his owner.

TRAINING BEGINS: ASK THE DOG A QUESTION

In order to teach your dog anything, you must first get his

Command your Brittany to sit using an authoritative tone of voice while raising your food hand over his head.

a foot short of him and hold out the treat as you ask, "School?" He will see you approaching with a treat in your hand and most likely begin walking toward you. As you meet, give him the treat and praise again.

The third time, ask the question, have a treat in your hand and walk only a short distance toward the dog so that he must walk almost all the way to you. As he reaches you, give him the treat and praise again.

By this time, the dog will probably be getting the idea that if he pays attention to you, especially when you ask that question, it will pay off in treats and enjoyable activities for him. In other words, he learns that "School" means doing great things with you that are fun and result in positive attention for him.

Remember that the dog does not understand your verbal language; he only recognizes sounds. Your question translates to a series of sounds for him, and those sounds become the signal to go to you and pay attention; if he does, he will get to interact with you plus receive treats and praise.

attention. After all, he cannot learn anything if he is looking away from you with his mind on something else.

To get his attention, ask him "School?" and immediately walk over to him and give him a treat as you tell him "Good dog." Wait a minute or two and repeat the routine, this time with a treat in your hand as you approach within a foot of the dog. Do not go directly to him, but stop about

THE BASIC COMMANDS

TEACHING SIT
Now that you have the dog's attention, attach his lead and

hold it in your left hand and a food treat in your right. Place your food hand at the dog's nose and let him lick the treat but not take it from you. Say "Sit" and slowly raise your food hand from in front of the dog's nose up over his head so that he is looking at the ceiling. As he bends his head upward, he will have to bend his knees to maintain his balance. As he bends his knees, he will assume a sit position. At that point, release the food treat and praise lavishly with comments such as "Good dog! Good sit!" Remember to always praise enthusiastically, because dogs relish verbal praise from their owners and feel so proud of themselves whenever they accomplish a behavior.

   You will not use food forever in getting the dog to obey your commands. Food is only used to teach new behaviors, and once the dog knows what you want when you give a specific command, you will wean him off the food treats but still maintain the verbal praise. After all, you will always have your voice with you, and there will be many times when you have no food rewards but expect the dog to obey.

TEACHING DOWN
Teaching the down exercise is easy when you understand how the dog perceives the down position, and it is very difficult when

you do not. Dogs perceive the down position as a submissive one; therefore, teaching the down exercise using a forceful method can sometimes make the dog develop such a fear of the down that he either runs away when you say "Down" or he attempts to snap at the person who tries to force him down.

   Have the dog sit close along-side your left leg, facing in the same direction as you are. Hold the lead in your left hand and a food treat in your right. Now

If the Brittany is not responding to your voice command and gesture, you may have to give him a little hands-on encouragement.

DOUBLE JEOPARDY

A dog in jeopardy never lies down. He stays alert on his feet because instinct tells him that he may have to run away or fight for his survival. Therefore, if a dog feels threatened or anxious, he will not lie down. Consequently, it is important to keep the dog calm and relaxed as he learns the down exercise.

Now place the food hand at the dog's nose, say "Down" very softly (almost a whisper) and slowly lower the food hand to the dog's front feet. When the food hand reaches the floor, begin moving it forward along the floor in front of the dog. Keep talking softly to the dog, saying things like, "Do you want this treat? You can do this, good dog." Your reassuring tone of voice will help calm the dog as he tries to follow the food hand in order to get the treat.

When the dog's elbows touch the floor, release the food and praise softly. Try to get the dog to maintain that down position for several seconds before you let him sit up again. The goal here is to get the dog to settle down and not feel threatened in the down position.

Once your dog has learned the down, you can progress to the down/stay. Many trainers use a combination of verbal commands and hand signals.

place your left hand lightly on the top of the dog's shoulders where they meet above the spinal cord. Do not push down on the dog's shoulders; simply rest your left hand there so you can guide the dog to lie down close to your left leg rather than to swing away from your side when he drops.

TEACHING STAY

It is easy to teach the dog to stay in either a sit or a down position. Again, we use food and praise during the teaching process as we help the dog to understand exactly what it is that we are expecting him to do.

To teach the sit/stay, start with the dog sitting on your left side as before and hold the lead in your left hand. Have a food treat in your right hand and place your food hand at the dog's nose. Say "Stay" and step out on your right foot to stand directly in front of the dog, toe to toe, as he licks and nibbles the treat. Be sure to keep his head facing upward to maintain the sit position. Count to five and then swing around to stand next to the dog again with him on your

left. As soon as you get back to the original position, release the food and praise lavishly.

To teach the down/stay, do the down as previously described. As soon as the dog lies down, say "Stay" and step out on your right foot just as you did in the sit/stay. Count to five and then return to stand beside the dog with him on your left side. Release the treat and praise as always.

Within a week or ten days, you can begin to add a bit of distance between you and your

Once the dog recognizes the stay command, you can increase the distance between you as well as the length of time.

CONSISTENCY PAYS OFF

Dogs need consistency in their feeding schedule, exercise and relief visits, and in the verbal commands you use. If you use "Stay" on Monday and "Stay here, please" on Tuesday, you will confuse your dog. Don't demand perfect behavior during training sessions and then let him have the run of the house the rest of the day. Above all, lavish praise on your pet consistently every time he does something right. The more he feels he is pleasing you, the more willing he will be to learn.

"WHERE ARE YOU?"

When calling the dog, do not say "Come." Say things like, "Rover, where are you? See if you can find me! I have a biscuit for you!" Keep up a constant line of chatter with coaxing sounds and frequent questions such as, "Where are you?" The dog will learn to follow the sound of your voice to locate you and receive his reward.

hand and quickly learn that he is going to get that treat as soon as you return to his side.

When you can stand 1 yard away from your dog for 30 seconds, you can then begin building time and distance in both stays. Eventually, the dog can be expected to remain in the stay position for prolonged periods of time until you return to him or call him to you. Always praise lavishly when he stays.

TEACHING COME

If you make teaching "come" an exciting experience, you should never have a student that does not love the game or that fails to come when called. The secret, it seems, is never to teach the word "come."

At times when an owner most wants his dog to come when called, the owner is likely to be upset or anxious and he allows these feelings to come through in the tone of his voice when he calls his dog. Hearing that desperation in his owner's voice, the dog fears the results of going to him and therefore either disobeys outright or runs in the opposite direction. The secret, therefore, is to teach the dog a game and, when you want him to come to you, simply play the game. It is practically a no-fail solution!

To begin, have several members of your family take a

dog when you leave him. When you do, use your left hand open with the palm facing the dog as a stay signal, much the same as the hand signal a police officer uses to stop traffic at an intersection. Hold the food treat in your right hand as before, but this time the food is not touching the dog's nose. He will watch the food

few food treats and each go into a different room in the house. Take turns calling the dog, and each person should celebrate the dog's finding him with a treat and lots of happy praise. When a person calls the dog, he is actually inviting the dog to find him and get a treat as a reward for "winning."

A few turns of the "Where are you?" game and the dog will understand that everyone is playing the game and that each person has a big celebration awaiting his success at locating them. Once he learns to love the game, simply calling out "Where are you?" will bring him running from wherever he is when he hears that all-important question.

The come exercise is recognized as one of the most important things to teach a dog, but there are trainers who work with thousands of dogs and never teach the actual word "come." Yet these dogs will race to respond to a

person who uses the dog's name followed by "Where are you?" For example, a woman has a 12-year-old companion dog who went blind, but who never fails to locate her owner when asked, "Where are you?"

Children, in particular, love to play this game with their dogs. Children can hide in smaller places like a shower stall or bathtub, behind a bed or under a table. The dog needs to work a little bit harder to find these hiding places, but when he does he loves to celebrate with a treat and a tussle with a favorite youngster.

TEACHING HEEL

Heeling means that the dog walks beside the owner without pulling. It takes time and patience on the owner's part to succeed at teaching the dog that he (the owner) will not proceed unless the dog is walking calmly beside him. Pulling out ahead on the lead is definitely not acceptable.

Begin by holding the lead in your left hand as the dog sits beside your left leg. Move the loop end of the lead to your right hand but keep your left hand short on the lead so it keeps the dog in close next to you.

Say "Heel" and step forward on your left foot. Keep the dog close to you and take three steps. Stop and have the dog sit next to

"COME" . . . BACK

Never call your dog to come to you for a correction or scold him when he reaches you. That is the quickest way to turn a come command into "Go away fast!" Dogs think only in the present tense, and your dog will connect the scolding with coming to you, not with the misbehavior of a few moments earlier.

HEELING WELL

Teach your dog to heel in an enclosed area. Once you think the dog will obey reliably and you want to attempt advanced obedience exercises such as off-lead heeling, test him in a fenced-in area so he cannot run away.

stopping, at which point the dog is told to sit again.

Your goal here is to have the dog walk those three steps without pulling on the lead. Once he will walk calmly beside you for three steps without pulling, increase the number of steps you take to five. When he will walk politely beside you while you take five steps, you can increase the length of your walk to ten steps. Keep increasing the length of your stroll until the dog will walk quietly beside you without pulling as long as you want him to heel. When you stop heeling, indicate to the dog that the exercise is over by verbally praising as you pet him and say "OK, good dog." The "OK" is used as a release word, meaning that the exercise is finished and the dog is free to relax.

If you are dealing with a dog who insists on pulling you around, simply "put on your brakes" and stand your ground until the dog realizes that the two of you are not going anywhere until he is beside you and moving at your pace, not his. It may take some time just standing there to convince the dog that you are the leader and you will be the one to decide on the direction and speed of your travel.

Each time the dog looks up at you or slows down to give a slack lead between the two of

you in what we now call the heel position. Praise verbally, but do not touch the dog. Hesitate a moment and begin again with "Heel," taking three steps and

you, quietly praise him and say, "Good heel. Good dog." Eventually, the dog will begin to respond and within a few days he will be walking politely beside you without pulling on the lead. At first, the training sessions should be kept short and very positive; soon the dog will be able to walk nicely with you for increasingly longer distances. Remember also to give the dog free time and the opportunity to run and play when you have finished heel practice.

WEANING OFF FOOD IN TRAINING

Food is used in training new behaviors. Once the dog understands what behavior goes with a specific command, it is time to start weaning him off the food treats. At first, give a treat after each exercise. Then, start to give a treat only after every other exercise. Mix up the times when you offer a food reward and the times when you only offer praise

so that the dog will never know when he is going to receive both food and praise and when he is going to receive only praise. This is called a variable-ratio-reward system and it proves successful because there is always the chance that the owner will produce a treat, so the dog never stops trying for that reward. No matter what, *always* give verbal praise.

Praise your Brittany for every good behavior. Your Brittany should want to obey you simply to please you—not to get a liver treat!

KEEP SMILING
Never train your dog, puppy or adult, when you are angry or in a sour mood. Dogs are very sensitive to human feelings, especially anger, and if your dog senses that you are angry or upset, he will connect your anger with his training and learn to resent or fear his training sessions.

OBEDIENCE CLASSES

It is a good idea to enroll in an obedience class if one is available in your area. If yours is a show dog, handling classes would be more appropriate. Many areas have dog clubs that offer basic obedience training as well as preparatory classes for obedience competition. There are also local dog trainers who offer similar classes.

At obedience trials, dogs can earn titles at various levels of competition. The beginning levels of competition include basic behaviors such as sit, down, heel, etc. The more advanced levels of competition include jumping, retrieving, scent discrimination and signal work. The advanced levels require a dog and owner to put a lot of time and effort into their training and the titles that can be earned at these levels of competition are very prestigious.

OTHER ACTIVITIES FOR LIFE

Whether a dog is trained in the structured environment of a class or alone with his owner at home, there are many activities that can bring fun and rewards to both owner and dog once they have mastered basic control. Teaching

Treats are used often in the show ring to get and hold the dog's attention as he stands for examination by the judge.

HOW TO WEAN THE "TREAT HOG"

If you have trained your dog by rewarding him with a treat each time he performs a command, he may soon decide that without the treat, he won't sit, stay or come. The best way to fix this problem is to start asking your dog to do certain commands twice before being rewarded. Slowly increase the number of commands given and then vary the number: three sits and a treat one day, five sits for a biscuit the next day, etc. Your dog will soon realize that there is no set number of sits before he gets his reward and he'll likely do it the first time you ask in the hope of being rewarded sooner rather than later.

For a basic water retrieve, the dog's attention is focused on the dummy as the trainer draws back to throw it.

OBEDIENCE SCHOOL

Taking your dog to an obedience school may be the best investment in time and money you can ever make. You will enjoy the benefits for the lifetime of your dog and you will have the opportunity to meet people who have similar expectations for companion dogs.

the dog to help out around the home, in the field or on the farm provides great satisfaction to both dog and owner. In addition, the dog's help makes life a little easier for his owner and raises his stature as a valued companion to his family. It helps give the dog a purpose by occupying his mind and providing an outlet for his energy.

Backpacking is an exciting and healthy activity that the dog can be taught without assistance from more than his owner. The exercise of walking and climbing is good for man and dog alike, and the bond that they develop together is priceless. The rule for backpacking with any dog is never to expect the dog to carry more than one-sixth of his body weight.

If you are interested in participating in organized competition with your Brittany, there are activities other than obedience in which you and your dog can

The dog watches as the dummy lands in the water.

The Brittany jumps into the water and...

...he's off after the dummy.

With dummy in mouth, the dog swims toward shore.

Once on land, the dog heads back to the trainer to return the dummy.

become involved. The Brittany naturally excels in hunting activities, including field trials, hunt tests and weekend trips with his family afield. For organized events, contact the American Kennel Club for rules and regulations plus a schedule of events. Agility is a popular sport where dogs run through an obstacle course that includes various jumps, tunnels and other exercises to test the dog's speed and coordination. The owners run beside their dogs to give commands and to guide them through the course. Although competitive, the focus is on fun— it's fun to do, fun to watch and great exercise.

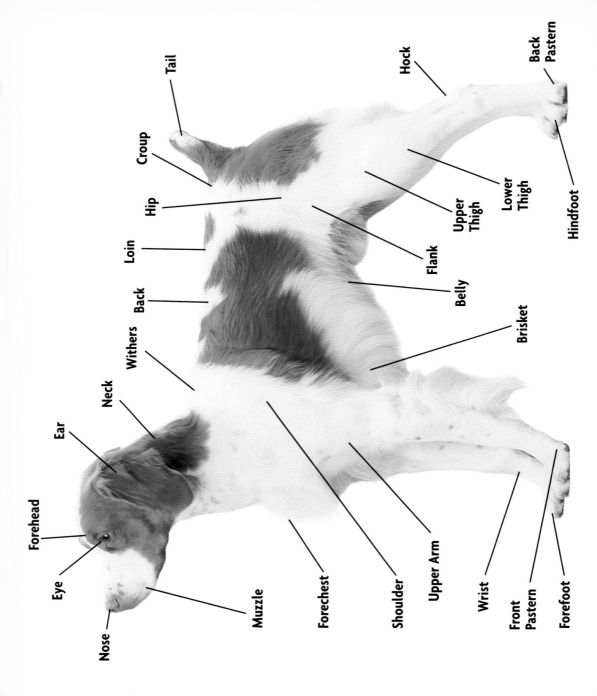

Physical Structure of the Brittany

HEALTH CARE OF YOUR

BRITTANY

Dogs suffer from many of the same physical illnesses as people. They might even share many of the same psychological problems. Since people usually know more about human diseases than canine maladies, many of the terms used in this chapter will be familiar but not necessarily those used by veterinarians. We will use the term *x-ray*, instead of the more acceptable term *radiograph*. We will also use the familiar term *symptoms* even though dogs don't have symptoms, which are verbal descriptions of the patient's feelings; dogs have *clinical signs*. Since dogs can't speak, we have to look for clinical signs...but we still use the term *symptoms* in this book.

As a general rule, medicine is *practiced*. That term is not arbitrary. Medicine is a constantly changing art as we learn more and more about genetics, electronic aids (like CAT scans and

MRIs) and daily laboratory advances. There are many dog maladies, like canine hip dysplasia, that are not universally treated in the same manner. Some veterinarians opt for surgery more often than others do.

SELECTING A VETERINARIAN

Your selection of a veterinarian should be based not only upon personality and ability with Sporting dogs but also upon his convenience to your home. You want a vet who is close because you might have emergencies or need to make multiple visits for treatments. You want a vet who has services that you might require such as boarding and grooming, as well as sophisticated pet supplies and a good reputation for ability and responsiveness. There is nothing more frustrating than having to wait a day or more to get a response from your veterinarian.

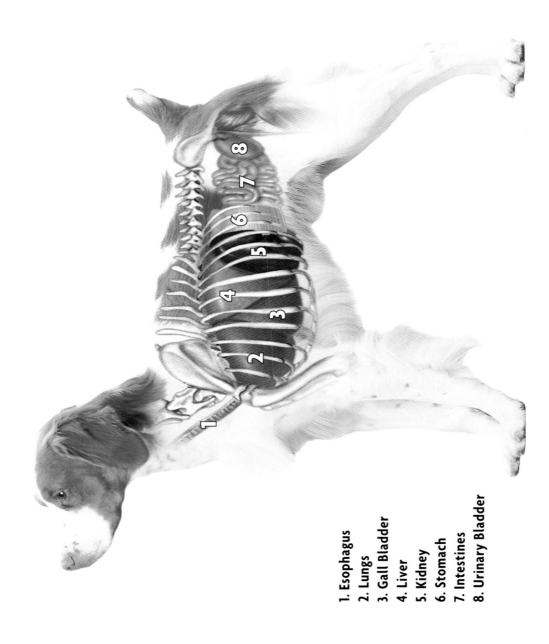

1. Esophagus
2. Lungs
3. Gall Bladder
4. Liver
5. Kidney
6. Stomach
7. Intestines
8. Urinary Bladder

Internal Organs of the Brittany

All veterinarians are licensed and their diplomas and/or certificates should be displayed in their waiting rooms. There are, however, many veterinary specialties that usually require further studies and internships. There are specialists in heart problems (veterinary cardiologists), skin problems (veterinary dermatologists), teeth and gum problems (veterinary dentists), eye problems (veterinary ophthalmologists) and x-rays (veterinary radiologists), as well as vets who have specialties in bones, muscles or certain organs. Most veterinarians do routine surgery such as neutering, stitching up wounds and docking tails for those breeds in which such is required for show purposes. When the problem affecting your dog is serious, it is not unusual or impudent to get another medical opinion, although it is

Breakdown of Veterinary Income by Category

2%	Dentistry
4%	Radiology
12%	Surgery
15%	Vaccinations
19%	Laboratory
23%	Examinations
25%	Medicines

A typical vet's income categorized according to services performed. This survey dealt with small-animal (pets) practices.

courteous to advise the vets concerned about this. You might also want to compare costs among several veterinarians. Sophisticated health care and veterinary services can be very costly. Important decisions often are influenced by financial considerations.

PREVENTATIVE MEDICINE
It is much easier, less costly and more effective to practice preventative medicine than to fight bouts of illness and disease. Properly bred puppies come from parents who were selected based upon their genetic-disease profile. Their mothers should have been vaccinated, free of all internal and external parasites and properly nourished. For these reasons, a visit to the veterinarian who

NEUTERING/SPAYING
Male dogs are castrated. The operation removes both testicles and requires that the dog be anesthetized. Recovery takes about one week. Females are spayed; in this operation, the uterus (womb) and both of the ovaries are removed. This is major surgery, also carried out under general anesthesia, and it usually takes a bitch two weeks to recover.

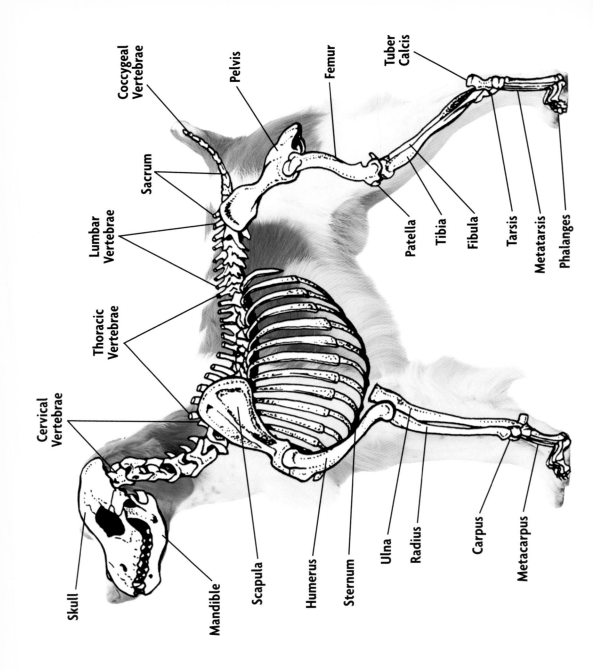

Coccygeal
Vertebrae

Pelvis

Femur

Tuber
Calcis

Sacrum

Patella

Tibia

Fibula

Tarsis

Metatarsis

Phalanges

Lumbar
Vertebrae

Thoracic
Vertebrae

Cervical
Vertebrae

Skull

Mandible

Scapula

Humerus

Sternum

Ulna

Radius

Carpus

Metacarpus

Skeletal Structure of the Brittany

cared for the dam is recommended. The dam can pass on disease resistance to her puppies, which can last for eight to ten weeks. She can also pass on parasites and many infections. That's why you should learn as much about the dam's health as possible.

VACCINATION SCHEDULING
Most vaccinations are given by injection and should only be done by a veterinarian. Both you and he should keep a record of the date of the injection, the identification of the vaccine and the amount given. Some vets give a first vaccination at eight weeks, but most dog breeders prefer the course not to commence until about ten weeks because of negating any antibodies passed on by the dam. The vaccination scheduling is usually based on a 15-day cycle. You must take your vet's advice regarding when to vaccinate as this may differ according to the

VACCINE ALLERGIES
Vaccines do not work all the time. Sometimes dogs are allergic to them and many times the antibodies, which are supposed to be stimulated by the vaccine, just are not produced. You should keep your dog in the veterinary clinic for an hour after it is vaccinated to be sure there are no allergic reactions.

vaccine used. Most vaccinations immunize your puppy against viruses.

The usual vaccines contain immunizing doses of several different viruses such as distemper, parvovirus, parainfluenza and hepatitis, although some veterinarians recommend separate vaccines for each disease. There are other vaccines available when the puppy is at risk. You should rely upon professional advice. This is especially true for the booster-shot program. Most vaccination programs require a booster when the puppy is a year old and once a year thereafter. In some cases, circumstances may require more or less frequent immunizations. Canine cough, more formally known as tracheobronchitis, is treated with a vaccine that is sprayed into the dog's nostrils. Canine cough is usually included in routine vaccination,

MORE THAN VACCINES
Vaccinations help prevent your new puppy from contracting diseases, but they do not cure them. Proper nutrition as well as parasite control keep your dog healthy and less susceptible to many dangerous diseases. Remember that your dog depends on you to ensure his well-being.

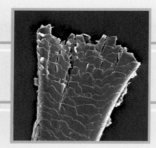
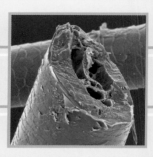

Normal hairs of a dog enlarged 200 times original size. The cuticle (outer covering) is clean and healthy. Unlike human hair that grows from the base, a dog's hair also grows from the end. Damaged hairs and split ends, illustrated above.

but this is often not so effective as for other major diseases.

WEANING TO FIVE MONTHS OLD
Puppies should be weaned by the time they are about two months old. A puppy that remains for at least eight weeks with his dam and littermates usually adapts better to other dogs and people later in life.

Some new owners have their puppy examined by a veterinarian immediately, which is a good idea. Vaccination programs usually begin when the puppy is very young.

The puppy will have his teeth examined and have his skeletal conformation and general health checked prior to certification by the veterinarian.

Puppies in certain breeds have problems with their kneecaps, cataracts and other eye problems, heart murmurs and undescended testicles. They may also have personality problems, and your veterinarian might have training in temperament evaluation.

Discuss a vaccination schedule with your veterinarian. Provide documentation from the breeder so that the vet can resume the schedule.

FIVE TO TWELVE MONTHS OF AGE
Unless you intend to breed or show your dog, neutering the puppy at six months of age is recommended. Discuss this with your veterinarian. Neutering has proven to be extremely beneficial to both bitches and dogs. Besides eliminating the possibility of pregnancy and pyometra in bitches and testicular cancer in male dogs, it inhibits (but does not prevent) breast cancer

PARVO FOR THE COURSE

Canine parvovirus is an highly contagious disease that attacks puppies and older dogs. Spread through contact with infected feces, parvovirus causes bloody diarrhea, vomiting, heart damage, dehydration, shock and death. To prevent this tragedy, breeders have their puppies begin their series of vaccinations at six to eight weeks of age. Be aware that the virus is easily spread and is carried on a dog's hair, feet, water bowls and other objects, as well as on people's shoes and clothing.

in bitches and prostate cancer in male dogs. Under no circumstances should a bitch be spayed prior to her first season.

Your veterinarian should provide your puppy with a thorough dental evaluation at six months of age, ascertaining whether all of the permanent teeth have erupted properly. A home dental-care regimen should be initiated at six months, including brushing weekly and providing good dental devices (such as nylon bones). Regular dental care promotes healthy teeth, fresh breath and a longer life.

OVER ONE YEAR OF AGE

Once a year, your grown dog should visit the vet for an examination and vaccination boosters, if needed. Some vets recommend blood tests, thyroid level check and dental evaluation to accompany these annual visits. A thorough clinical evaluation by the vet can provide critical background information for your dog. Blood tests are often performed at one year of age, and dental examinations around the third or fourth birthday. In the long run, quality preventative care for your pet can save money, teeth and lives.

HEALTH AND VACCINATION SCHEDULE

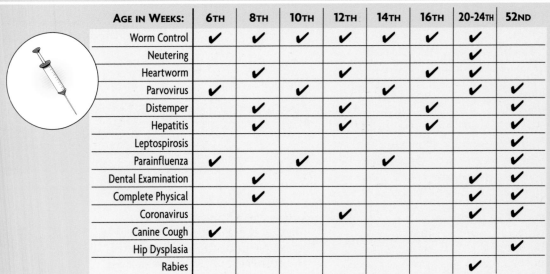

Age in Weeks:	6th	8th	10th	12th	14th	16th	20-24th	52nd
Worm Control	✔	✔	✔	✔	✔	✔	✔	
Neutering							✔	
Heartworm		✔		✔		✔	✔	
Parvovirus	✔		✔		✔		✔	✔
Distemper		✔		✔		✔		✔
Hepatitis		✔		✔		✔		✔
Leptospirosis								✔
Parainfluenza	✔		✔		✔			✔
Dental Examination		✔					✔	✔
Complete Physical		✔					✔	✔
Coronavirus				✔			✔	✔
Canine Cough	✔							
Hip Dysplasia								✔
Rabies							✔	

Vaccinations are not instantly effective. It takes about two weeks for the dog's immune system to develop antibodies. Most vaccinations require annual booster shots. Your vet should guide you in this regard.

SKIN PROBLEMS IN BRITTANYS

Veterinarians are consulted by dog owners for skin problems more than for any other group of diseases or maladies. Dogs' skin is almost as sensitive as human skin and both suffer from almost the same ailments (though the occurrence of acne in dogs is rare!). For this reason, veterinary dermatology has developed into a specialty practiced by many veterinarians.

Since many skin problems have visual symptoms that are almost identical, it requires the skill of an experienced veterinary dermatologist to identify and cure many of the more severe skin disorders. Pet shops sell many treatments for skin problems but most of the treatments are directed at symptoms and not the underlying problem(s). If your dog is suffering from a skin disorder, you should seek professional assistance as quickly as possible. As with all diseases, the earlier a problem is identified and treated, the more successful is the cure.

HEREDITARY SKIN DISORDERS

Veterinary dermatologists are currently researching a number of skin disorders that are believed to have hereditary bases. These inherited diseases are transmitted by both parents, who appear (phenotypically)

DENTAL HEALTH

A dental examination is in order when the dog is between six months and one year of age so that any permanent teeth that have erupted incorrectly can be corrected. It is important to begin a brushing routine at home, using dental-care products made for dogs, such as special toothbrushes and toothpaste. Durable nylon and safe edible chews should be a part of your puppy's arsenal for good health, good teeth and pleasant breath. The vast majority of dogs three to four years old and older has diseases of the gums from lack of dental attention. Using the various types of dental chews can be very effective in controlling dental plaque.

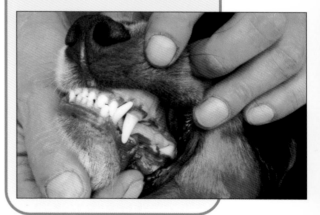

normal but have a recessive gene for the disease, meaning that they carry, but are not affected by, the disease. These diseases pose serious problems to breeders because in some instances there is no method of identifying carriers. Often the secondary diseases associated with these skin conditions are even more debilitating than the disorder itself, including cancers and respiratory problems.

Among the hereditary skin disorders, for which the mode of inheritance is known, are: color dilution alopecia, acrodermatitis, cutaneous asthenia (Ehlers-Danlos syndrome), sebaceous adenitis, cyclic hematopoiesis, dermatomyositis, IgA deficiency and nodular dermatofibrosis. Some of these disorders are limited to one or two breeds and others affect a large number of breeds. All inherited diseases must be diagnosed and treated by a veterinary specialist.

PARASITE BITES
Many of us are allergic to insect bites. The bites itch, erupt and may even become infected. Dogs have the same reaction to fleas, ticks and/or mites. When an insect lands on you, you have the chance to whisk it away with your hand. Unfortunately, when your dog is bitten by a flea, tick or mite, he can only scratch it away or bite it. By the time the dog has been bitten, the parasite has done some of its damage. It may also have laid eggs to cause further problems in the near future. The itching from parasite bites is probably due to the saliva injected into the site when the parasite sucks the dog's blood.

AUTO-IMMUNE SKIN CONDITIONS
Auto-immune skin conditions are commonly referred to as being allergic to yourself, while allergies are usually inflammatory reactions to an outside stimulus. Auto-immune diseases cause serious damage to the tissues that are involved.

The best known auto-immune disease is lupus, which affects people as well as dogs. The symptoms are variable and may affect the kidneys, bones,

A SKUNKY PROBLEM

Have you noticed your dog dragging his rump along the floor? If so, it is likely that his anal sacs are impacted or possibly infected. The anal sacs are small pouches located on both sides of the anus under the skin and muscles. They are about the size and shape of a grape and contain a foul-smelling liquid. Their contents are usually emptied when the dog has a bowel movement but, if not emptied completely, they will impact, which will cause your dog much pain. Fortunately, your veterinarian can tend to this problem easily by draining the sacs for the dog. Be aware that your dog might also empty his anal sacs in cases of extreme fright.

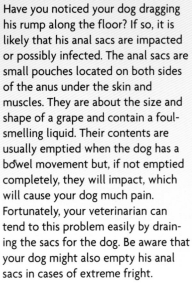

blood chemistry and skin. It can be fatal to both dogs and humans, though it is not thought to be transmissible. It is usually successfully treated with cortisone, prednisone or a similar corticosteroid, but extensive use of these drugs can have harmful side effects.

ACRAL LICK GRANULOMA

Many dogs have a very poorly understood syndrome called acral lick granuloma. The manifestation of the problem is the dog's tireless attack at a specific area of the body, almost always the legs or paws. The dog licks so intensively that he removes the hair and skin, leaving an ugly, large wound. Tiny protuberances, which are outgrowths of new capillaries, bead on the surface of the wound. Owners who notice their dogs' biting and chewing at their extremities should have the vet determine the cause. If lick granuloma is identified, although there is no absolute cure, corticosteroids are the most common treatment.

AIRBORNE ALLERGIES

Just as humans have hay fever, rose fever and other allergies from which they suffer during the pollinating season, many dogs suffer from the same allergies. When the pollen count is high, your dog might suffer but don't expect him to sneeze and

> ### "P" STANDS FOR PROBLEM
> Urinary tract disease is a serious condition that requires immediate medical attention. Symptoms include urinating in inappropriate places or the need to urinate frequently in small amounts. Urinary-tract disease is most effectively treated with antibiotics. To help promote good urinary-tract health, owners must always be sure that a constant supply of fresh water is available to their pets.

have a runny nose as a human would. Dogs react to pollen allergies the same way they react to fleas—they scratch and bite themselves. Dogs, like humans, can be tested for allergens. Discuss the testing with your veterinary dermatologist.

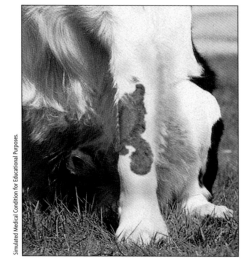

Simulated Medical Condition for Educational Purposes.

Acral lick is a poorly understood problem in which the dog licks incessantly at an area on of one of his legs, creating an open wound or "hot spot."

DISEASE REFERENCE CHART

	What is it?	What causes it?	Symptoms
Leptospirosis	Severe disease that affects the internal organs; can be spread to people.	A bacterium, which is often carried by rodents, that enters through mucous membranes and spreads quickly throughout the body.	Range from fever, vomiting and loss of appetite in less severe cases to shock, irreversible kidney damage and possibly death in most severe cases.
Rabies	Potentially deadly virus that infects warm-blooded mammals.	Bite from a carrier of the virus, mainly wild animals.	1st stage: dog exhibits change in behavior, fear. 2nd stage: dog's behavior becomes more aggressive. 3rd stage: loss of coordination, trouble with bodily functions.
Parvovirus	Highly contagious virus, potentially deadly.	Ingestion of the virus, which is usually spread through the feces of infected dogs.	Most common: severe diarrhea. Also vomiting, fatigue, lack of appetite.
Canine cough	Contagious respiratory infection.	Combination of types of bacteria and virus. Most common: *Bordetella bronchiseptica* bacteria and parainfluenza virus.	Chronic cough.
Distemper	Disease primarily affecting respiratory and nervous system.	Virus that is related to the human measles virus.	Mild symptoms such as fever, lack of appetite and mucus secretion progress to evidence of brain damage, "hard pad."
Hepatitis	Virus primarily affecting the liver.	Canine adenovirus type I (CAV-1). Enters system when dog breathes in particles.	Lesser symptoms include listlessness, diarrhea, vomiting. More severe symptoms include "blue-eye" (clumps of virus in eye).
Coronavirus	Virus resulting in digestive problems.	Virus is spread through infected dog's feces.	Stomach upset evidenced by lack of appetite, vomiting, diarrhea.

FOOD PROBLEMS

FOOD ALLERGIES
Dogs can be allergic to many foods that are best-sellers and highly recommended by breeders and veterinarians. Changing the brand of food that you buy may not eliminate the problem if the element to which the dog is allergic is contained in the new brand.

Recognizing a food allergy is difficult. Humans vomit or have rashes when they eat a food to which they are allergic. Dogs neither vomit nor (usually) develop a rash. They react in the same manner as they do to an airborne or flea allergy; they itch, scratch and bite, thus making the diagnosis extremely difficult. While pollen allergies and parasite bites are usually seasonal, food allergies are year-round problems.

FOOD INTOLERANCE
Food intolerance is the inability of the dog to completely digest

certain foods. Puppies that may have done very well on their mother's milk, for example, may not do well on cow's milk. The result of this food intolerance may be loose bowels, passing gas and stomach pains. These are the only obvious symptoms of food intolerance, which makes diagnosis difficult.

TREATING FOOD PROBLEMS

It is possible to handle food allergies and food intolerance yourself. Put your dog on a diet that he has never had. Obviously if he has never eaten this new food, he can't have been allergic or intolerant of it. Start with a single ingredient that is not in the dog's diet at the present time. Ingredients like chopped beef or chicken are common in dogs' diets, so try something more exotic like rabbit, pheasant or another source of quality protein. Keep the dog on this diet (with no additives) for a month. If the symptoms of food allergy or intolerance disappear, chances are your dog has a food allergy.

Don't think that the single ingredient cured the problem. You still must find a suitable diet and ascertain which ingredient in the old diet was objectionable. This is most easily done by adding ingredients to the new diet one at a time. Let the dog stay on the modified diet for a month before you add

PET ADVANTAGES
If you do not intend to show or breed your new puppy, your veterinarian will probably recommend that you spay your female or neuter your male. Some people believe neutering leads to weight gain, but if you feed and exercise your dog properly, this is easily avoided. Spaying or neutering can actually have many positive outcomes, such as:
- training becomes easier, as the dog focuses less on the urge to mate and more on you!
- females are protected from unplanned pregnancy as well as ovarian and uterine cancers.
- males are guarded from testicular tumors and have a reduced risk of developing prostate cancer.
   Talk to your vet regarding the right age to spay/neuter and other aspects of the procedure.

another ingredient. Eventually, you will determine the ingredient that caused the adverse reaction.

An alternative method is to carefully study the ingredients in the diet to which your dog is allergic or intolerant. Identify the main ingredient in this diet and eliminate it by buying a different food that does not have that ingredient. Keep experimenting until the symptoms disappear after one month on the new diet.

A male dog flea,
Ctenocephalides
canis.

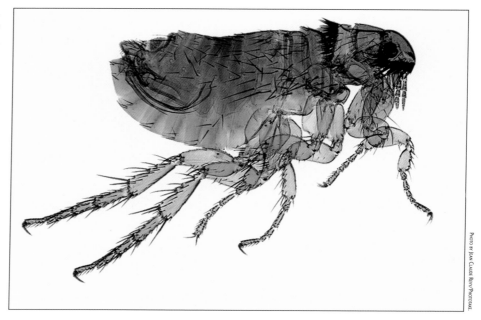

EXTERNAL PARASITES

FLEAS

Of all the problems to which dogs are prone, none is more well known and frustrating than fleas. Flea infestation is relatively simple to cure but difficult to prevent. Parasites that are harbored inside the body are a bit more difficult to eradicate but they are easier to control.

To control flea infestation, you have to understand the flea's life cycle. Fleas are often thought of as a summertime problem, but centrally heated homes have changed the patterns and fleas can be found at any time of the year. The most effective method of flea control is a two-stage approach: one stage to kill the adult fleas, and the other to control the development of pre-adult fleas. Unfortunately, no single active ingredient is effective against all stages of the life cycle.

FLEA KILLER CAUTION— "POISON"

Flea-killers are poisonous. You should not spray these toxic chemicals on areas of a dog's body that he licks, including his genitals and his face. Flea killers taken internally are a better answer, but check with your vet in case internal therapy is not advised for your dog.

LIFE CYCLE STAGES

During its life, a flea will pass through four life stages: egg, larva, pupa or nymph and adult. The adult stage is the most visible and irritating stage of the flea life cycle, and this is why the majority of flea-control products concentrate on this stage. The fact is that adult fleas account for only 1% of the total flea population, and the other 99% exist in pre-adult stages, i.e., eggs, larvae and nymphs. The pre-adult stages are barely visible to the naked eye.

THE LIFE CYCLE OF THE FLEA

Eggs are laid on the dog, usually in quantities of about 20 or 30, several times a day. The adult female flea must have a blood meal before each egg-laying session. When first laid, the eggs will cling to the dog's hair, as the eggs are still moist. However, they will quickly dry out and fall from the dog, especially if the dog moves around or scratches. Many eggs will fall off in the dog's favorite area or an area in which he spends a lot of time, such as his bed.

Once the eggs fall from the dog onto the carpet or furniture, they will hatch into larvae. This takes from one to ten days. Larvae are not particularly mobile and will usually travel only a few inches from where they hatch. However, they do have a tendency to move away from bright light and heavy

---

EN GARDE:
CATCHING FLEAS OFF GUARD!
Consider the following ways to arm yourself against fleas:
- Add a small amount of pennyroyal or eucalyptus oil to your dog's bath. These natural remedies repel fleas.
- Supplement your dog's food with fresh garlic (minced or grated) and a hearty amount of brewer's yeast, both of which ward off fleas.
- Use a flea comb on your dog daily. Submerge fleas in a cup of bleach to kill them quickly.
- Confine the dog to only a few rooms to limit the spread of fleas in the home.
- Vacuum daily...and get all of the crevices! Dispose of the bag every few days until the problem is under control.
- Wash your dog's bedding daily. Cover cushions where your dog sleeps with towels, and wash the towels often.

---

traffic—under furniture and behind doors are common places to find high quantities of flea larvae.

The flea larvae feed on dead organic matter, including adult flea feces, until they are ready to change into adult fleas. Fleas will usually remain as larvae for around seven days. After this period, the larvae will pupate into protective pupae. While inside the pupae, the larvae will undergo

Fleas have been measured as being able to jump 300,000 times and can jump over 150 times their length in any direction, including straight up.

metamorphosis and change into adult fleas. This can take as little time as a few days, but the adult fleas can remain inside the pupae waiting to hatch for up to two years. The pupae are signaled to hatch by certain stimuli, such as physical pressure—the pupae's being stepped on, heat from an animal's lying on the pupae or increased carbon-dioxide levels and vibrations—indicating that a suitable host is available.

Once hatched, the adult flea must feed within a few days. Once the adult flea finds a host, it will not leave voluntarily. It only becomes dislodged by grooming or the host animal's scratching.

The adult flea will remain on the host for the duration of its life unless forcibly removed.

TREATING THE ENVIRONMENT AND THE DOG

Treating fleas should be a two-pronged attack. First, the environment needs to be treated; this includes carpets and furniture, especially the dog's bedding and areas underneath furniture. The environment should be treated with a household spray containing an Insect Growth Regulator (IGR) and an insecticide to kill the adult fleas. Most IGRs are effective against eggs and larvae; they actually mimic the fleas' own hormones and stop the eggs and larvae from developing into adult fleas. There are currently no treatments available to attack the pupa stage of the life cycle, so the adult insecticide is used to kill the newly hatched adult fleas before they find a host. Most IGRs are active for many months, while

A scanning electron micrograph of a dog or cat flea, *Ctenocephalides*, magnified more than 100x. This image has been colorized for effect.

THE LIFE CYCLE OF THE FLEA

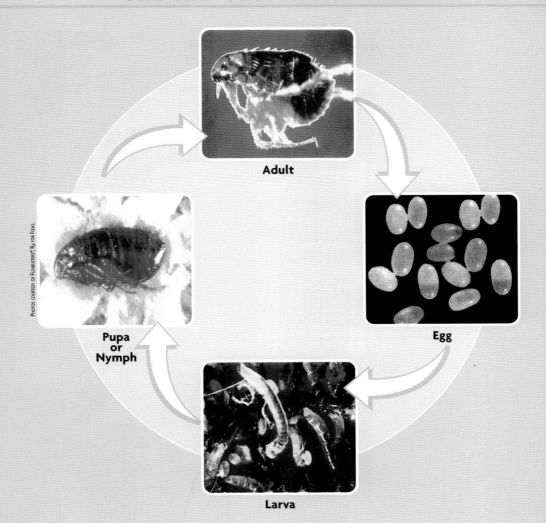

Adult

Egg

Larva

Pupa
or
Nymph

PHOTOS COURTESY OF FLEABUSTERS®, Rx FOR FLEAS.

A LOOK AT FLEAS
Fleas have been around for millions of years and have adapted to changing host animals. They are able to go through a complete life cycle in less than one month or they can extend their lives to almost two years by remaining as pupae or cocoons. They do not need blood or any other food for up to 20 months.

INSECT GROWTH REGULATOR (IGR)

Two types of products should be used when treating fleas—a product to treat the pet and a product to treat the home. Adult fleas represent less than 1% of the flea population. The pre-adult fleas (eggs, larvae and pupae) represent more than 99% of the flea population and are found in the environment; it is in the case of pre-adult fleas that products containing an Insect Growth Regulator (IGR) should be used in the home.

IGRs are a new class of compounds used to prevent the development of insects. They do not kill the insect outright, but instead use the insect's biology against it to stop it from completing its growth. Products that contain methoprene are the world's first and leading IGRs. Used to control fleas and other insects, this type of IGR will stop flea larvae from developing and protect the house for up to seven months.

The American dog tick, *Dermacentor variabilis*, is probably the most common tick found on dogs. Look at the strength in its eight legs! No wonder it's hard to detach them.

adult insecticides are only active for a few days.

When treating with a household spray, it is a good idea to vacuum before applying the product. This stimulates as many pupae as possible to hatch into adult fleas. The vacuum cleaner should also be treated with an insecticide to prevent the eggs and larvae that have been collected in the vacuum bag from hatching.

The second stage of treatment is to apply an adult insecticide to the dog. Traditionally, this would be in the form of a collar or a spray, but more recent innovations include digestible insecticides that poison the fleas when they ingest the dog's blood. Alternatively, there are drops that, when placed on the back of the dog's neck, spread throughout the dog's hair and skin to kill adult fleas.

TICKS

Though not as common as fleas, ticks are found all over the tropical and temperate world. They don't bite, like fleas; they harpoon. They dig their sharp proboscis (nose) into the dog's skin and drink the blood. Their

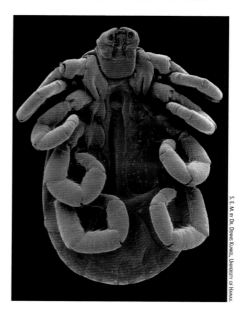

S. E. M. BY DR. DENNIS KUNKEL, UNIVERSITY OF HAWAII

only food and drink is dog's blood. Dogs can get Lyme disease, Rocky Mountain spotted fever, tick bite paralysis and many other diseases from ticks. They may live where fleas are found and they like to hide in cracks or seams in walls. They are controlled the same way fleas are controlled.

The American dog tick, *Dermacentor variabilis*, may well be the most common dog tick in many geographical areas, especially those areas where the climate is hot and humid. Most dog ticks have life expectancies of a week to six months, depending upon climatic conditions. They can neither jump nor fly, but they can crawl slowly and can range up to 16 feet to reach a sleeping or unsuspecting dog.

MITES

Just as fleas and ticks can be problematic for your dog, mites can also lead to an itchy nuisance. Microscopic in size, mites are related to ticks and generally take up permanent residence on their host animal—in this case, your dog! The term *mange* refers to any infestation caused by one of the mighty mites, of which there are six varieties that concern dog owners.

Demodex mites cause a condition known as demodicosis

DEER-TICK CROSSING

The great outdoors may be fun for your dog, but it also is home to dangerous ticks. Deer ticks carry a bacterium known as *Borrelia burgdorferi* and are most active in the autumn and spring. When infections are caught early, penicillin and tetracycline are effective antibiotics, but, if left untreated, the bacteria may cause neurological, kidney and cardiac problems as well as long-term trouble with walking and painful joints.

S.E.M. BY DR. ANDREW SPIELMAN/PHOTOTAKE.

PHOTO BY DR. DENNIS KUNKEL, UNIVERSITY OF HAWAII.

The head of an American dog tick, *Dermacentor variabilis*, enlarged and colorized for effect.

PHOTO BY JAMES HAYDEN/YOAV/PHOTOTAKE.

(sometimes called red mange or follicular mange), in which the mites live in the dog's hair follicles and sebaceous glands in larger-than-normal amounts. This type of mange is commonly passed from the dam to her puppies and usually shows up on the puppies' muzzles, though demodicosis is not transferable from one normal dog to another. Most dogs recover from this type of mange without any treatment, though topical therapies are commonly prescribed by the vet.

The *Cheyletiellosis* mite is the hook-mouthed culprit associated with "walking dandruff," a condition that affects dogs as well as cats and rabbits. This mite lives on the surface of the animal's skin and is readily transferable through direct or indirect contact with an affected animal. The dandruff is present in the form of scaly skin, which may or may not be itchy. If not treated, this mange can affect a whole kennel of dogs and can be spread to humans as well.

The *Sarcoptes* mite causes intense itching on the dog in the form of a condition known as scabies or sarcoptic mange. The cycle of the *Sarcoptes* mite lasts about three weeks, and the mites live in the top layer of the dog's skin (epidermis), preferably in areas with little hair. Scabies is highly contagious and can be passed to humans. Sometimes an allergic reaction to the mite worsens the severe itching associated with sarcoptic mange.

Ear mites, *Otodectes cynotis,* lead to otodectic mange, which most commonly affects the outer ear canal of the dog, though other areas can be affected as well. Dogs with ear-mite infestation commonly scratch at their ears, causing further irritation, and shake their heads. Dark brown droppings in the outer ear confirm the diagnosis. Your vet can prescribe a treatment to flush out the ears and kill any eggs in the ears. A complete month of treatment is necessary to cure the mange.

Two other mites, less common in dogs, include *Dermanyssus gallinae* (the poultry or red mite) and *Eutrombicula alfreddugesi* (the North American mite associated with trombiculidiasis or chigger infestation). The poultry mite frequently lives on chickens, but can transfer to dogs who spend time near farm animals. Chigger infestation affects dogs in the

DO NOT MIX
Never mix parasite-control products without first consulting your vet. Some products can become toxic when combined with others and can cause fatal consequences.

NOT A DROP TO DRINK
Never allow your dog to swim in polluted water or public areas where water quality can be suspect. Even perfectly clear water can harbor parasites, many of which can cause serious to fatal illnesses in canines. Areas inhabited by waterfowl and other wildlife are especially dangerous.

central US who have exposure to woodlands. The types of mange caused by both of these mites are treatable by veterinarians.

INTERNAL PARASITES

Most animals—fishes, birds and mammals, including dogs and humans—have worms and other parasites that live inside their bodies. According to Dr. Herbert R. Axelrod, the fish pathologist, there are two kinds of parasites: dumb and smart. The smart parasites live in peaceful cooperation with their hosts (symbiosis), while the dumb parasites kill their hosts. Most worm infections are relatively easy to control. If they are not controlled, they weaken the host dog to the point that other medical problems occur, but they do not kill the host as dumb parasites would.

A brown dog tick, *Rhipicephalus sanguineus,* is an uncommon but annoying tick found on dogs.
PHOTO BY CAROLINA BIOLOGICAL SUPPLY/PHOTOTAKE.

The roundworm *Rhabditis* can infect both dogs and humans.

ROUNDWORMS

Average-size dogs can pass 1,360,000 roundworm eggs every day. For example, if there were only 1 million dogs in the world, the world would be saturated with thousands of tons of dog feces. These feces would contain around 15,000,000,000 roundworm eggs.

Up to 31% of home yards and children's sand boxes in the US contain roundworm eggs.

Flushing dog's feces down the toilet is not a safe practice because the usual sewage treatments do not destroy roundworm eggs.

Infected puppies start shedding roundworm eggs at three weeks of age. They can be infected by their mother's milk.

The roundworm, *Ascaris lumbricoides*.

ROUNDWORMS

The roundworms that infect dogs are known scientifically as *Toxocara canis*. They live in the dog's intestines and shed eggs continually. It has been estimated that a dog produces about 6 or more ounces of feces every day. Each ounce of feces averages hundreds of thousands of roundworm eggs. There are no known areas in which dogs roam that do not contain roundworm eggs. The greatest danger of roundworms is that they infect people, too! It is wise to have your dog tested regularly for roundworms.

In young puppies, roundworms cause bloated bellies, diarrhea, coughing and vomiting, and are transmitted from the dam (through blood or milk). Affected puppies will not appear as animated as normal puppies. The worms appear spaghetti-like, measuring as long as 6 inches. Adult dogs can acquire roundworms through coprophagia (eating contaminated feces) or by killing rodents that carry roundworms.

Roundworm infection can kill puppies and cause severe problems in adults, as the hatched larvae travel to the lungs and trachea through the bloodstream. Cleanliness is the best preventative for roundworms. Always pick up after your dog and dispose of feces in appropriate receptacles.

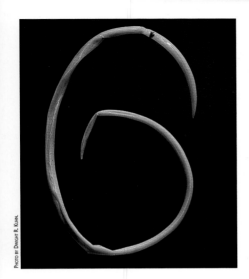

PHOTO BY DWIGHT R. KUHN.

HOOKWORMS

In the United States, dog owners have to be concerned about four different species of hookworm, the most common and most serious of which is *Ancylostoma caninum,* which prefers warm climates. The others are *Ancylostoma braziliense, Ancylostoma tubaeforme* and *Uncinaria stenocephala,* the latter of which is a concern to dogs living in the northern US and Canada, as this species prefers cold climates. Hookworms are dangerous to humans as well as to dogs and cats, and can be the cause of severe anemia due to iron deficiency. The worm uses its teeth to attach itself to the dog's intestines and changes the site of its attachment about six times per day. Each time the worm repositions itself, the dog loses blood and can become anemic. *Ancylostoma caninum* is the most likely of the four species to cause anemia in the dog.

Symptoms of hookworm infection include dark stools, weight loss, general weakness, pale coloration and anemia, as well as possible skin problems. Fortunately, hookworms are easily purged from the affected dog with a number of medications that have proven effective. Discuss these with your veterinarian. Most heartworm preventatives include a hookworm insecticide as well.

Owners also must be aware that hookworms can infect humans, who can acquire the larvae through exposure to contaminated feces. Since the worms cannot complete their life cycle on a human, the worms simply infest the skin and cause irritation. This condition is known as cutaneous larva migrans syndrome. As a preventative, use disposable gloves or a "poop-scoop" to pick up your dog's droppings and prevent your dog (or neighborhood cats) from defecating in children's play areas.

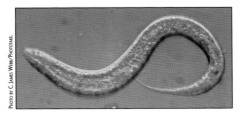

PHOTO BY C. JAMES WEBB/PHOTOTAKE.

The infective stage of the hookworm larva.

TAPEWORMS

Humans, rats, squirrels, foxes, coyotes, wolves and domestic dogs are all susceptible to tapeworm infection. Except in humans, tapeworms are usually not a fatal infection. Infected individuals can harbor 1000 parasitic worms.

Tapeworms, like some other types of worm, are hermaphroditic, meaning male and female in the same worm.

If dogs eat infected rats or mice, or anything else infected with tapeworm, they get the tapeworm disease. One month after attaching to a dog's intestine, the worm starts shedding eggs. These eggs are infective immediately. Infective eggs can live for a few months without a host animal.

The head and rostellum (the round prominence on the scolex) of a tapeworm, which infects dogs and humans.

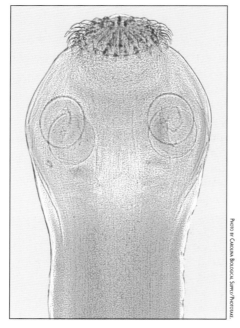

PHOTO BY CAROLINA BIOLOGICAL SUPPLY/PHOTOTAKE.

TAPEWORMS

There are many species of tapeworm, all of which are carried by fleas! The most common tapeworm affecting dogs is known as *Dipylidium caninum*. The dog eats the flea and starts the tapeworm cycle. Humans can also be infected with tapeworms—so don't eat fleas! Fleas are so small that your dog could pass them onto your hands, your plate or your food and thus make it possible for you to ingest a flea that is carrying tapeworm eggs.

While tapeworm infection is not life-threatening in dogs (smart parasite!), it can be the cause of a very serious liver disease for humans. About 50% of the humans infected with *Echino-coccus multilocularis*, a type of tapeworm that causes alveolar hydatid, perish.

WHIPWORMS

In North America, whipworms are counted among the most common parasitic worms in dogs. The whipworm's scientific name is *Trichuris vulpis*. These worms attach themselves in the lower parts of the intestine, where they feed. Affected dogs may only experience upset tummies, colic and diarrhea. These worms, however, can live for months or years in the dog, beginning their larval stage in the small intestine, spending their adult stage in the large intestine and finally passing infective eggs through the dog's feces. The only way to detect whipworms is through a fecal examination, though this is not always foolproof. Treatment for whipworms is tricky, due to the worms' unusual life-cycle pattern, and very often dogs are reinfected due to exposure to infective eggs on the ground. The whipworm eggs can survive in the environment for as long as five years; thus, cleaning up droppings in your own backyard as well as in public places is absolutely essential for sanitation purposes and the health of your dog and others.

THREADWORMS
Though less common than round-worms, hookworms and those previously mentioned, threadworms concern dog owners in the south-western US and Gulf Coast area, where the climate is hot and humid. Living in the small intestine of the dog, this worm measures a mere 2 millimeters and is round in shape. Like that of the whipworm, the threadworm's life cycle is very complex and the eggs and larvae are passed through the feces. A deadly disease in humans, *Strongyloides* readily infects people, and the handling of feces is the most common means of transmission. Threadworms are most often seen in young puppies; bloody diarrhea and pneumonia are symptoms. Sick puppies must be isolated and treated immediately; vets recommend a follow-up treatment one month later.

HEARTWORM PREVENTATIVES

There are many heartworm preventatives on the market, many of which are sold at your veterinarian's office. These products can be given daily or monthly, depending on the manufacturer's instructions. All of these preventatives contain chemical insecticides directed at killing heartworms, which leads to some controversy among dog owners. In effect, heartworm preventatives are necessary evils, though you should determine how necessary based on your pet's lifestyle. There is no doubt that heartworm is a dreadful disease that threatens the lives of dogs. However, the likelihood of your dog's being bitten by an infected mosquito is slim in most places, and a mosquito-repellent (or an herbal remedy such as Wormwood or Black Walnut) is much safer for your dog and will not compromise his immune system (the way heartworm preventatives will). Should you decide to use the traditional preventative "medications," you can consider giving the pill every other or third month. Since the toxins in the pill will kill the heartworms at all stages of development, the pill would be effective in killing larvae, nymphs or adults and it takes four months for the larvae to reach the adult stage. Thus, there is no rationale to poisoning the dog's system on a monthly basis. Lastly, do not give the pill during the winter months since there are no mosquitoes around to pass on their infection, unless you live in a tropical environment.

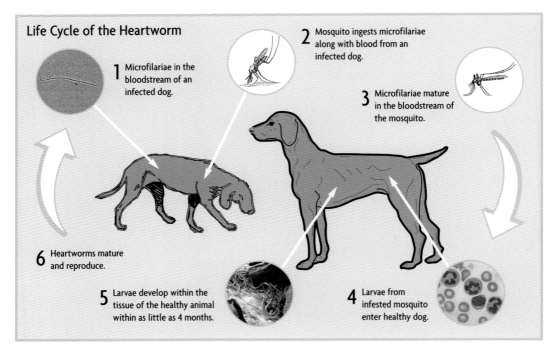

Life Cycle of the Heartworm

1 Microfilariae in the bloodstream of an infected dog.

2 Mosquito ingests microfilariae along with blood from an infected dog.

3 Microfilariae mature in the bloodstream of the mosquito.

4 Larvae from infested mosquito enter healthy dog.

5 Larvae develop within the tissue of the healthy animal within as little as 4 months.

6 Heartworms mature and reproduce.

HEARTWORMS

Heartworms are thin, extended worms up to 12 inches long, which live in a dog's heart and the major blood vessels surrounding it. Dogs may have up to 200 worms. Symptoms may be loss of energy, loss of appetite, coughing, the development of a pot belly and anemia.

Heartworms are transmitted by mosquitoes. The mosquito drinks the blood of an infected dog and takes in larvae with the blood. The larvae, called microfilariae, develop within the body of the mosquito and are passed on to the next dog bitten after the larvae

mature. It takes two to three weeks for the larvae to develop to the infective stage within the body of the mosquito. Dogs are usually treated at about six weeks of age and maintained on a prophylactic dose given monthly.

Blood testing for heartworms is not necessarily indicative of how seriously your dog is infected. Although this is a dangerous disease, it is not easy for a dog to be infected. Discuss the various preventatives with your vet, as there are many different types now available. Together you can decide on a safe course of prevention for your dog.

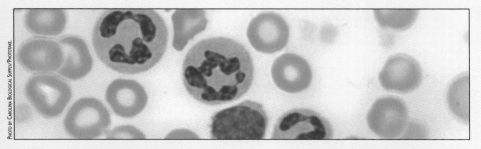

Magnified heartworm larvae, *Dirofilaria immitis.*

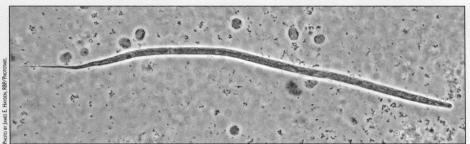

Heartworm, *Dirofilaria immitis.*

The heart of a dog infected with canine heartworm, *Dirofilaria immitis.*

Number-One Killer Disease in Dogs: CANCER

In every age, there is a word associated with a disease or plague that causes humans to shudder. In the 21st century, that word is "cancer." Just as cancer is the leading cause of death in humans, it claims nearly half the lives of dogs that die from a natural disease as well as half the dogs that die over the age of ten years.

Described as a genetic disease, cancer becomes a greater risk as the dog ages. Vets and dog owners have become increasingly aware of the threat of cancer to dogs. Statistics reveal that one dog in every five will develop cancer, the most common of which is skin cancer. Many cancers, including prostate, ovarian and breast cancer, can be avoided by spaying and neutering our dogs by the age of six months.

Early detection of cancer can save or extend a dog's life, so it is absolutely vital for owners to have their dogs examined by a qualified vet or oncologist immediately upon detection of any abnormality. Certain dietary guidelines have also proven to reduce the onset and spread of cancer. Foods based on fish rather than beef, due to the presence of Omega-3 fatty acids, are recommended. Other amino acids such as glutamine have significant benefits for canines, particularly those breeds that show a greater susceptibility to cancer.

Cancer management and treatments promise hope for future generations of canines. Since the disease is genetic, breeders should never breed a dog whose parents, grandparents and any related siblings have developed cancer. It is difficult to know whether to exclude an otherwise healthy dog from a breeding program, as the disease does not manifest itself until the dog's senior years.

RECOGNIZE CANCER WARNING SIGNS

Since early detection can possibly rescue your dog from becoming a cancer statistic, it is essential for owners to recognize the possible signs and seek the assistance of a qualified professional.

- Abnormal bumps or lumps that continue to grow
- Bleeding or discharge from any body cavity
- Persistent stiffness or lameness
- Recurrent sores or sores that do not heal
- Inappetence
- Breathing difficulties
- Weight loss
- Bad breath or odors
- General malaise and fatigue
- Eating and swallowing problems
- Difficulty urinating and defecating

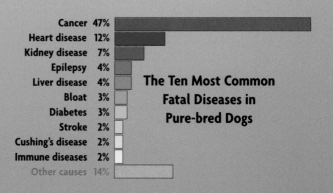

Disease	%
Cancer	47%
Heart disease	12%
Kidney disease	7%
Epilepsy	4%
Liver disease	4%
Bloat	3%
Diabetes	3%
Stroke	2%
Cushing's disease	2%
Immune diseases	2%
Other causes	14%

The Ten Most Common Fatal Diseases in Pure-bred Dogs

Recognizing a Sick Dog

Unlike colicky babies and cranky children, our canine kids cannot tell us when they are feeling ill. Therefore, there are a number of signs that owners can identify to know that their dogs are not feeling well.

Take note for physical manifestations such as:

- unusual, bad odor, including bad breath
- excessive shedding
- wax in the ears, chronic ear irritation
- oily, flaky, dull haircoat
- mucus, tearing or similar discharge in the eyes
- fleas or mites
- mucus in stool, diarrhea
- sensitivity to petting or handling
- licking at paws, scratching face, etc.

Keep an eye out for behavioral changes as well including:

- lethargy, idleness
- lack of patience or general irritability
- lack of interest in food
- phobias (fear of people, loud noises, etc.)
- strange behavior, suspicion, fear
- coprophagia
- more frequent barking
- whimpering, crying

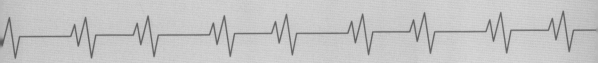

Get Well Soon

You don't need a DVM to provide good TLC to your sick or recovering dog, but you do need to pay attention to some details that normally wouldn't bother him. The following tips will aid Fido's recovery and get him back on his paws again:

- Keep his space free of irritating smells, like heavy perfumes and air fresheners.
- Rest is the best medicine! Avoid harsh lighting that will prevent your dog from sleeping. Shade him from bright sunlight during the day and dim the lights in the evening.
- Keep the noise level down. Animals are more sensitive to sound when they are sick.

- Be attentive to any necessary temperature adjustments. A dog with a fever needs a cool room and cold liquids. A bitch that is whelping or recovering from surgery will be more comfortable in a warm room, consuming warm liquids and food.
- You wouldn't send a sick child back to school early, so don't rush your dog back into a full routine until he seems absolutely ready.

The term *old* is a qualitative term. For dogs, as well as their masters, old is relative. Certainly we can all distinguish between a puppy Brittany and an adult Brittany—there are the obvious physical traits, such as size, appearance and facial expressions, and personality traits. Puppies and young dogs like to play with children. Children's natural exuberance is a good match for the seemingly endless energy of young dogs. They like to run, jump, chase and retrieve. When dogs grow older and cease their interaction with children, they are often thought of as being too old to play with the young people.

On the other hand, if a Brittany is only exposed to people with quieter lifestyles, his life will normally be less active and he will not seem to be getting old as his activity level slows down.

If people live to be 100 years old, dogs live to be 20 years old. While this is a

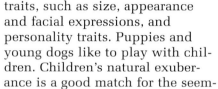

Brittanys show their age by slowing down and resting more, not unlike older humans; they may even suffer from some of the same age-related problems.

good rule of thumb, it is very inaccurate. When trying to compare dog years to human years, you cannot make a generalization about all dogs. You can make the generalization that 12 or 13 years is a good lifespan for a Brittany, which is quite good compared to many other pure-bred dogs that may only live to 8 or 9 years of age. Dogs are generally considered mature within three years, but they can reproduce even earlier. So the first three years of a dog's life are like seven times that of comparable humans. That means a 3-year-old dog is like a 21-year-old human. As the curve of comparison shows, there is no hard and fast rule for comparing dog and human ages. The comparison is made even more difficult, for not all humans age at the same rate...and human females live longer than human males.

WHAT TO LOOK FOR IN SENIORS

Most veterinarians and behaviorists use the seven-year mark as the time to consider a dog a senior. The term *senior* does not imply that the dog is geriatric and has begun to fail in mind and body. Aging is essentially a slowing process. Humans readily admit that they feel a difference in their activity level from age 20 to 30, and then from 30 to 40, etc. By treating the seven-year-old dog as

a senior, owners are able to implement certain therapeutic and preventative medical strategies with the help of their veterinarians. A senior-care program should include at least two veterinary visits per year, screening sessions to determine the dog's health

GETTING OLD

An old dog starts to show one or more of the following symptoms:

- Sleep patterns are deeper and longer and the old dog is harder to awaken.

- Food intake diminishes.

- Responses to calls, whistles and other signals are ignored more and more.

- Eye contacts do not evoke tail wagging.

- The hair on his face and paws starts to turn gray. The color breakdown usually starts around the eyes and mouth.

The bottom line is simply that a dog is getting old when you think he is getting old because he slows down in his general activities, including walking, running, eating, jumping and retrieving. On the other hand, certain activities increase, like more sleeping, more barking and more repetition of habits like going to the door when you put your coat on without being called.

status and nutritional counseling. Veterinarians determine the senior dog's health status through a blood smear for a complete blood count, serum chemistry profile with electrolytes, urinalysis, blood pressure check, electrocardiogram, ocular tonometry (pressure on the eyeball) and dental prophylaxis.

Such an extensive program for senior dogs is well advised before owners start to see the obvious physical signs of aging, such as slower and inhibited movement, graying, increased sleep/nap periods and disinterest in play and other activity. This preventative program promises a longer, healthier life for the aging dog. Among the physical problems

common in aging dogs are the loss of sight and hearing, arthritis, kidney and liver failure, diabetes mellitus, heart disease, and Cushing's disease (a hormonal disease).

In addition to the physical manifestations discussed, there are some behavioral changes and problems related to aging dogs. Dogs suffering from hearing or vision loss, dental discomfort or arthritis can become aggressive. Likewise, the near-deaf and/or blind dog may be startled more easily and react in an unexpectedly aggressive manner. Seniors suffering from senility can become more impatient and irritable. Housesoiling accidents are associated with loss of mobility, kidney

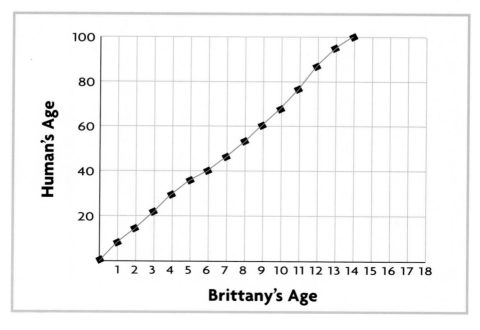

CDS: COGNITIVE DYSFUNCTION SYNDROME
"Old-Dog Syndrome"

There are many ways for you to evaluate old-dog syndrome. Veterinarians have defined CDS (cognitive dysfunction syndrome) as the gradual deterioration of cognitive abilities. These are indicated by changes in the dog's behavior. When a dog changes his routine response, and maladies have been eliminated as the cause of these behavioral changes, then CDS is the usual diagnosis.

More than half the dogs over eight years old suffer from some form of CDS. The older the dog, the more chance he has of suffering from CDS. In humans, doctors often dismiss the CDS behavioral changes as part of "winding down."

There are four major signs of CDS: frequent potty accidents inside the home, sleeping much more or much less than normal, acting confused and failing to respond to social stimuli.

SYMPTOMS OF CDS

FREQUENT POTTY ACCIDENTS
- *Urinates in the house.*
- *Defecates in the house.*
- *Doesn't signal that he wants to go out.*

SLEEP PATTERNS
- *Awakens more slowly.*
- *Sleeps more than normal during the day.*
- *Sleeps less during the night.*

CONFUSION
- *Goes outside and just stands there.*
- *Appears confused with a faraway look in his eyes.*
- *Hides more often.*
- *Doesn't recognize friends.*
- *Doesn't come when called.*
- *Walks around listlessly and without a destination.*

FAILURE TO RESPOND TO SOCIAL STIMULI
- *Comes to people less frequently, whether called or not.*
- *Doesn't tolerate petting for more than a short time.*
- *Doesn't come to the door when you return home.*

NOTICING THE SYMPTOMS

The symptoms listed below are symptoms that gradually appear and become more noticeable. They are not life-threatening; however, the symptoms below are to be taken very seriously and warrant a discussion with your veterinarian:

- Your dog cries and whimpers when he moves, and he stops running completely.
- Convulsions start or become more serious and frequent. The usual convulsion (spasm) is when the dog stiffens and starts to tremble, being unable or unwilling to move. The seizure usually lasts for 5 to 30 minutes.
- Your dog drinks more water and urinates more frequently. Wetting and bowel accidents take place indoors without warning.
- Vomiting becomes more and more frequent.

problems and loss of sphincter control as well as plaque accumulation, physiological brain changes and reactions to medications. Older dogs, just like young puppies, suffer from separation anxiety, which can lead to excessive barking, whining, housesoiling and destructive behavior. Seniors may become fearful of everyday sounds, such as vacuum cleaners, heaters, thunder and passing traffic. Some dogs have difficulty sleeping, due to discomfort, the need for frequent potty visits and the like.

Owners should avoid spoiling the older dog with too many fatty treats. Obesity is a common problem in older dogs and subtracts years from their lives. Keep the senior dog as trim as possible since excessive weight puts additional stress on the body's vital organs. Some breeders recommend supplementing the diet with foods high in fiber and lower in calories. Adding fresh vegetables and marrow broth to the senior's diet makes a tasty, low-calorie, low-fat supplement. Vets also offer specialty diets for senior dogs that are worth exploring.

Your dog, as he nears his twilight years, needs his owner's patience and good care more than ever. Never punish an older dog for an accident or abnormal behavior. For all the years of love, protection and companion-

EUTHANASIA SERVICES
Euthanasia must be done by a licensed vet, who may be considerate enough to come to your home. There also may be societies for the prevention of cruelty to animals in your area. They often offer this service upon a vet's recommendation.

ship that your dog has provided, he deserves special attention and courtesies. The older dog may need to relieve himself at 3 a.m. because he can no longer hold it for eight hours. Older dogs may not be able to remain crated for more than two or three hours. It may be time to give up a sofa or chair to your old friend. Although he may not seem as enthusiastic about your attention and petting, he does appreciate the considerations you offer as he gets older.

Your Brittany does not understand why his world is slowing down. Owners must make the transition into the golden years as pleasant and rewarding as possible.

WHAT TO DO WHEN THE TIME COMES

You are never fully prepared to make a rational decision about putting your dog to sleep. It is very obvious that you love your Brittany or you would not be reading this book. Putting a loved

dog to sleep is extremely difficult. It is a decision that must be made with your veterinarian. You are usually forced to make the decision when one of the life-threatening symptoms listed above becomes serious enough for you to seek veterinary help.

If the prognosis of the malady indicates the end is near and your beloved pet will only suffer more and experience no enjoyment for the balance of his life, then euthanasia is the right choice.

WHAT IS EUTHANASIA?

Euthanasia derives from the Greek, meaning *good death*. In other words, it means the planned, painless killing of a dog suffering from a painful, incurable condition, or who is so aged that he cannot walk, see, eat or control his excretory functions.

Euthanasia is usually accomplished by injection with an overdose of an anesthesia or barbiturate. Aside from the prick of the needle, the experience is usually painless.

MAKING THE DECISION

The decision to euthanize your dog is never easy. The days during which the dog becomes ill and the end occurs can be unusually stressful for you. If this is your first experience with the death of a loved one, you may need the comfort dictated by your religious beliefs. If you are the head of the family and have children, you should involve them in the decision of putting your Brittany to sleep. Usually your dog can be maintained on drugs for a few days in order to give you ample time to make a decision. During this time, talking with members of your family or even people who have lived through this same experience can ease the burden of your inevitable decision.

Most urban areas have pet cemeteries located nearby. Your vet can probably help you locate one close to your home.

THE FINAL RESTING PLACE

Dogs can have some of the same privileges as humans. The remains of your beloved dog can

COPING WITH LOSS

When your dog dies, you may be as upset as when a human companion passes away. You are losing your protector, your baby, your confidante and your best friend. Many people experience not only grief but also feelings of guilt and doubt as to whether they did all that they could for their pet. Allow yourself to grieve and mourn, and seek help from friends and support groups. You may also wish to consult books and websites that deal with this topic.

be buried in a pet cemetery, which is generally expensive. Dogs who have died at home can be buried in your yard in a place suitably marked with some stone or newly planted tree or bush. Alternatively, they can be cremated individually and the ashes returned to you. A less expensive option is mass cremation, although, of course, the ashes can not then be returned. Vets can usually arrange the cremation on your behalf. The cost of these options should always be discussed frankly and openly with your veterinarian.

GETTING ANOTHER DOG?

The grief of losing your beloved dog will be as lasting as the grief of losing a human friend or relative. In most cases, if your dog died of old age (if there is such a thing), he had slowed down considerably. Do you want a new Brittany puppy to replace him? Or are you better off finding a more mature Brittany, say two to three years of age, which will usually be house-trained and will have an already developed personality. In this case, you can find out if you like each other after a few hours of being together.

The decision is, of course, your own. Do you want another Brittany or perhaps a different breed so as to avoid comparison with your beloved friend? Most people usually choose the same

breed because they know and love the characteristics of that breed. Then, too, they often know people who have the same breed and perhaps they are lucky enough that one of their friends expects a litter soon. What could be better?

Most pet cemeteries have facilities in which you can store your dog's ashes.

> ## TO THE RESCUE
> Some people choose to adopt or "rescue" an older dog instead of buying a new puppy. Some older dogs may have come from abusive environments and be fearful, while other dogs may have developed many bad habits; both situations can present challenges to their new owners. Training an older dog will take more time and patience, but persistence and an abundance of praise and love can transform a dog into a well-behaved, loyal companion.

BRITTANY

When you purchase your Brittany, you will make it clear to the breeder whether you want one just as a lovable companion and pet, or if you hope to be buying a Brittany with show prospects. No reputable breeder will sell you a young puppy and tell you that it is *definitely* of show quality, for so much can go wrong during the early months of a puppy's development. If you plan to show, what you will hopefully have acquired is a puppy with "show potential."

To the novice, exhibiting a Brittany in the show ring may look easy, but it takes a lot of hard work and devotion to do top winning at a show such as the prestigious Westminster Kennel Club dog show, not to mention a little luck too!

The first concept that the canine novice learns when watching a dog show is that each dog first competes against members of his own breed. Once the judge has selected the best member of each breed (Best of Breed), that chosen dog will compete with other dogs in his group. Finally, the dogs chosen first in each group will compete for Best in Show.

The second concept that you must understand is that the dogs are not actually compared against one another. The judge compares each dog against his breed standard, the American Kennel Club (AKC)-approved written description of the ideal breed specimen. While some early breed standards were

INFORMATION ON CLUBS

You can get information about dog shows from the national kennel clubs:

American Kennel Club
5580 Centerview Dr., Raleigh, NC 27606-3390
www.akc.org

United Kennel Club
100 E. Kilgore Road, Kalamazoo, MI 49002
www.ukcdogs.com

Canadian Kennel Club
89 Skyway Ave., Suite 100, Etobicoke, Ontario
M9W 6R4 Canada
www.ckc.ca

The Kennel Club
1-5 Clarges St., Piccadilly, London W1Y 8AB, UK
www.the-kennel-club.org.uk

indeed based on specific dogs that were famous or popular, many dedicated enthusiasts say that a perfect specimen, as described in the standard, has never walked into a show ring, has never been bred and, to the woe of dog breeders around the globe, does not exist. Breeders attempt to get as close to this ideal as possible with every litter, but theoretically the "perfect" dog is so elusive that it is impossible.

If you are interested in exploring the world of dog showing, your best bet is to join your local breed club or the national parent club, which is the American Brittany Club. These clubs host both regional and national specialties, shows only for Brittanys, which can include conformation as well as obedience and field trials. Even if you have no intention of competing with your Brittany, a specialty is like a festival for lovers of the breed who congregate to share their favorite topic: Brittanys! Clubs also send out newsletters, and some organize training days and seminars in order that people may learn more about their chosen breed. To locate the breed club closest to you, contact the AKC, which furnishes the rules and regulations for all of these events plus general dog registration and other basic requirements of dog ownership.

The AKC offers three kinds of conformation shows: an all-breed show (for all AKC-recognized breeds), a specialty show (for one breed only, usually sponsored by

BECOMING A CHAMPION

An official AKC champion of record requires that a dog accumulate 15 points under three different judges, including two "majors" under different judges. Points are awarded based on the number of dogs entered into competition, varying from breed to breed and place to place. A win of three, four or five points is considered a "major." The AKC annually assigns a schedule of points to adjust the variations that accompany a breed's popularity and the population of a given area.

PRACTICE AT HOME

If you have decided to show your dog, you must train him to gait around the ring by your side at the correct pace and pattern, and to tolerate being handled and examined by the judge. Most breeds require complete dentition, all breeds require a particular bite (scissors, level or undershot) and all males must have two apparently normal testicles fully descended into the scrotum. Enlist family and friends to hold mock trials in your yard to prepare your future champion!

the parent club) and a Group show (for all breeds in the Group).

For a dog to become an AKC champion of record, the dog must accumulate 15 points at the shows from at least three different judges, including two "majors." A "major" is defined as a three-, four- or five-point win. The number of points per win is determined by the number of dogs entered in the show on that day. Depending on the breed, the number of points that are awarded varies. At any dog show, only one dog and one bitch of each breed can win points.

Dog showing does not offer "co-ed" classes. Dogs and bitches never compete against each other in the classes. Non-champion dogs are called "class dogs"

because they compete in one of five classes. Dogs are entered in a particular class depending on their ages and previous show wins.

To begin, there is the Puppy Class (for 6- to 9-month-olds and for 9- to 12-month-olds); this class is followed by the Novice Class (for dogs that have not won any first prizes except in the Puppy Class or three first prizes in the Novice Class and have not accumulated any points toward their champion title); the Bred-by-Exhibitor Class (for dogs handled by their breeders or handled by one of the breeder's immediate family); the American-bred Class (for dogs bred in the US); and the Open Class (for any dog that is not a champion).

The judge begins judging the Puppy Class, first dogs and then bitches, and proceeds through the classes. The judge places his winners first through fourth in each class. In the next-level class, the Winners Class, the first-place winners of each class compete with one another to determine Winners Dog and Winners Bitch. The judge also places a Reserve Winners Dog and Reserve Winners Bitch, which could be awarded the points in the case of a disqualification. The Winners Dog and Winners Bitch, the two that are awarded the points for the breed, then compete with any champions of record entered in the show, called "specials." The judge reviews the Winners Dog, Winners Bitch and all of the champions to select his Best of Breed. The Best of Winners is selected between the Winners Dog and Winners Bitch. Were one of these two to be selected Best of Breed, he or she would automatically be named Best of Winners as well. Finally the judge selects his Best of Opposite Sex to the Best of Breed winner.

At a Group show or all-breed show, the Best of Breed winners from each breed then compete against one another in their respective groups for Group One through Group Four. The judge compares each Best of Breed to his breed standard, and the dog that most closely lives up to the ideal for his breed is selected as Group One. Finally, all seven group winners (from the Sporting Group, Toy Group, Hound Group, etc.) compete for Best in Show.

To find out about dog shows in your area, you can subscribe to the American Kennel Club's monthly magazine, the *American Kennel Gazette* and the accompanying *Events Calendar*. You can also look in your local newspaper for advertisements for dog shows in your area or go on the Internet to the AKC's website, www.akc.org.

SHOW QUALITY SHOWS

While you may purchase a puppy in the hope of having a successful career in the show ring, it is impossible to tell, at eight to ten weeks of age, whether your dog will be a contender. Some promising pups end up with minor to serious faults that prevent them from taking home an award, but this certainly does not mean they can't be the best of companions for you and your family. To find out if your potential show dog is show-quality, enter him in a match to see how a judge evaluates him. You may also take him back to your breeder as he matures to see what he might advise.

CANINE GOOD CITIZEN® PROGRAM

Have you ever considered getting your dog "certified"? The AKC's Canine Good Citizen® Program affords your dog just that opportunity. Your dog shows that he is a well-behaved canine citizen, using the basic training and good manners you have taught him, by taking a series of ten tests that illustrate that he can behave properly at home, in a public place and around other dogs. The tests are administered by participating dog clubs, colleges, 4-H clubs, scouts and other community groups and are open to all pure-bred and mixed-breed dogs. Upon passing the ten tests, the suffix CGC is then applied to your dog's name.

The ten tests are: 1. Accepting a friendly stranger; 2. Sitting politely for petting; 3. Appearance and grooming; 4. Walking on a lead; 5. Walking through a group of people; 6. Sit, down and stay on command; 7. Coming when called; 8. Meeting another dog; 9. Calm reaction to distractions; 10. Separation from owner.

If your Brittany is six months of age or older and registered with the AKC, you can enter him in a dog show where the breed is offered classes. Provided that your Brittany does not have a disqualifying fault, he can compete. Only unaltered dogs can be entered in a dog show, so if you have spayed or neutered your Brittany, he cannot compete in conformation shows. The reason for this is simple. Dog shows are the main forum to prove which representatives of a breed are worthy of being bred. Only dogs that have achieved championships—the AKC "seal of approval" for quality in pure-bred dogs—should be bred. Altered dogs, however, can participate in other AKC events such as obedience trials and the Canine Good Citizen program.

OBEDIENCE TRIALS

Obedience trials in the US trace back to the early 1930s when organized obedience training was developed to demonstrate how well dog and owner could work together. The pioneer of obedience trials is Mrs. Helen Whitehouse Walker, a Standard Poodle fancier, who designed a series of exercises after the Associated, Sheep, Police Army Dog Society of Great Britain. Since the days of Mrs. Walker, obedience trials have grown by leaps and bounds, and today there are over 2,000 trials held in the US every year, with more than 100,000 dogs competing. Any AKC-registered dog can enter an obedience trial, regardless of conformational disqualifications or neutering.

Obedience trials are divided into three levels of progressive difficulty. At the first level, the

Novice, dogs compete for the title Companion Dog (CD); at the intermediate level, the Open, dogs compete for the title Companion Dog Excellent (CDX); and at the advanced level, the Utility, dogs compete for the title Utility Dog (UD). Classes are sub-divided into "A" (for beginners) and "B" (for more experienced handlers). A perfect score at any level is 200, and a dog must score 170 or better to earn a "leg," of which three are needed to earn the title. To earn points, the dog must score more than 50% of the available points in each exercise; the possible points range from 20 to 40.

Each level consists of a different set of exercises. In the Novice level, the dog must heel on- and off-lead, come, long sit, long down and stand for exami-nation. These skills are the basic

NO SHOW

Never show a dog that is sick or recovering from surgery or infection. Not only will this put your own dog under a tremendous amount of stress, but you will also put other dogs at risk of contracting any illness your dog has. Likewise, bitches who are in heat will distract and disrupt the performances of males who are competing, and bitches that are preg-nant will likely be stressed and exhausted by a long day of showing.

ones required for a well-behaved "Companion Dog." The Open level requires that the dog perform the same exercises above, but without a leash, for extended lengths of time, as well as retrieve a dumbbell, broad jump and drop on recall. In the Utility level, dogs must perform ten difficult exercises, including scent discrimination, hand signals for basic commands, directed jump and directed retrieve.

Once a dog has earned the UD title, he can compete with other proven obedience dogs for the coveted title of Utility Dog Excellent (UDX), which requires

Show Brittanys have the desired appearance of elegant simplicity, never overly groomed or trimmed.

that the dog win "legs" in ten shows. Utility Dogs who earn "legs" in Open B and Utility B earn points toward their Obedience Trial Champion title. In 1977, the title Obedience Trial Champion (OTCh.) was established by the AKC. To become an OTCh., a dog needs to earn 100 points, which requires three first places in Open B and Utility under three different judges.

AGILITY TRIALS

Having had its origins in the UK back in 1977, AKC agility had its official beginning in August 1994, when the first licensed agility trials were held. The AKC allows all registered breeds (including Miscellaneous Class breeds) to participate, providing the dog is 12 months of age or older. Agility is designed so that the handler demonstrates how well the dog can work at his side. The handler directs his dog over an obstacle course that includes jumps as well as tires, the dog walk, weave poles, pipe tunnels, collapsed tunnels, etc. While working his way through the course, the dog must keep one eye and ear on the handler and the rest of his body on the course. The handler gives verbal commands and hand signals to guide the dog through the course.

TRACKING

Any dog is capable of tracking, using his nose to follow a trail. Tracking tests are exciting and competitive ways to test your Brittany's ability to search and rescue. The AKC started tracking tests in 1937, when the first AKC-licensed test took place as part of the Utility level at an obedience trial. Ten years later in 1947, the AKC offered the first title, Tracking Dog (TD). It was not until 1980 that the AKC added the Tracking Dog Excellent title (TDX), which was followed by the Versatile Surface Tracking title (VST) in 1995. The title Champion Tracker (CT) is awarded to a dog who has earned all three titles.

Whether a show dog, field dog or agility dog, the Brittany must move freely with good reach and drive.

FIELD TRIALS

Field trials are offered to the retrievers, pointers and spaniel breeds of the Sporting Group. The purpose of field trials is to demonstrate a dog's ability to perform his original purpose in the field. The events vary depending on the type of dog, but in all trials dogs compete against one another for placement and for points toward their Field Champion (FC) titles.

Brittanys run in pointing field trials along with other breeds like the Pointer, German Shorthair, Wirehair and Weimaraner. Pointing dogs must quarter the field, running in pairs over ground on which live birds are released. They must find the game and point it, be steady to wing and shot, then retrieve it to the hunter's hand upon command. Every field trial includes four stakes of increasing

Practice makes Brittanys fly! This handsome dog is practicing for an obedience trial.

JUNIOR SHOWMANSHIP

For budding dog handlers, ages 10 to 18 years, Junior Showmanship competitions are an excellent training ground for the next generation of dog professionals. Owning and caring for a dog are wonderful methods of teaching children responsibility, and Junior Showmanship builds upon that foundation. Juniors learn by grooming, handling and training their dogs, and the quality of junior's presentation of the dog (and himself) is being evaluated by a licensed judge. The junior can enter with any registered AKC dog to compete, including an ILP, provided that the dog lives with him or a member of his family.

Junior Showmanship competitions are divided into two classes: Novice (for beginners) and Open (for juniors show have three first place wins in the Novice Class). The junior must run with the dog with the rest of the handlers and dogs, stack the dog for examination and individually gait the dog in a specific pattern. Juniors should practice with a handling class or an experienced handler before entering the Novice Class so that they recognize all the jargon that the judge may use.

A National Junior Organization was founded in 1997 to help promote the sport of dog showing among young people. The AKC also offers a Junior Scholarship for juniors who excel in the program.

levels of difficulty. Each stake is judged by a team of two judges who look for many natural abilities including steadiness, courage, style, control and training.

HUNTING TESTS

Hunting tests are not competitive like field trials, and participating dogs are judged against a standard like in a conformation show. The first hunting tests were devised by the North American Hunting Retriever Association (NAHRA) as an alternative to field trials for retriever owners to appreciate their dogs' natural innate ability in the field without the expense and pressure of formal field trials. The intent of hunting tests is the same as that of field trials, to test the dog's ability in a simulated hunting scenario.

The AKC instituted its hunting tests in June 1985, and popularity has grown tremendously. The AKC offers three titles at hunting tests, Junior Hunter (JH), Senior Hunter (SH) and Master Hunter (MH). Each title requires that the dog earn qualifying "legs" at the tests: the JH requiring four; the SH, five; and the MH, six. In addition to the AKC, the United Kennel Club also offers hunting tests through its affiliate club, the Hunting Retriever Club, Inc. (HRC), which began the tests in 1984.

AMERICAN KENNEL CLUB TITLES

The AKC offers over 40 different titles to dogs in competition. Depending on the events that your dog can enter, different titles apply. Some titles can be applied as prefixes, meaning that they are placed before the dog's name (e.g., Ch. King of the Road) and others are used as suffixes, placed after the dog's name (e.g., King of the Road, CD).

These titles are used as prefixes:

Conformation Dog Shows
- Ch. (Champion)

Obedience Trials
- NOC (National Obedience Champion)
- OTCH (Obedience Trial Champion)
- VCCH (Versatile Companion Champion)

Tracking Tests
- CT [Champion Tracker (TD,TDX and VST)]

Agility Trials
- MACH (Master Agility Champion)
- MACH2, MACH3, MACH4, etc.

Field Trials
- FC (Field Champion)
- AFC (Amateur Field Champion)
- NFC (National Field Champion)
- NAFC (National Amateur Field Champion)
- NOGDC (National Open Gun Dog Champion)
- AKC GDSC (AKC Gun Dog Stake Champion)
- AKC RGDSC (AKC Retrieving Gun Dog Stake Champion)

Herding Trials
- HC (Herding Champion)

Dual
- DC (Dual Champion — Ch. and FC)

Triple
- TC (Triple Champion — Ch., FC and OTCH)

Coonhounds
- NCH (Nite Champion)
- GNCH (Grand Nite Champion)
- SHNCH (Senior Grand Nite Champion)
- GCH (Senior Champion)
- SGCH (Senior Grand Champion)
- GFC (Grand Field Champion)
- SGFC (Senior Grand Field Champion)
- WCH (Water Race Champion)
- GWCH (Water Race Grand Champion)
- SGWCH (Senior Grand Water Race Champion)

These titles are used as suffixes:

Obedience
- CD (Companion Dog)
- CDX (Companion Dog Excellent)
- UD (Utility Dog)
- UDX (Utility Dog Excellent)
- VCD1 (Versatile Companion Dog 1)
- VCD2 (Versatile Companion Dog 2)
- VCD3 (Versatile Companion Dog 3)
- VCD4 (Versatile Companion Dog 4)

Tracking Tests
- TD (Tracking Dog)
- TDX (Tracking Dog Excellent)
- VST (Variable Surface Tracker)

Agility Trials
- NA (Novice Agility)
- OA (Open Agility)
- AX (Agility Excellent)
- MX (Master Agility Excellent)
- NAJ (Novice Jumpers with weaves)
- OAJ (Open Jumpers with weaves)
- AXJ (Excellent Jumpers with weaves)
- MXJ (Master Excellent Jumpers with weaves)

Hunting Test
- JH (Junior Hunter)
- SH (Senior Hunter)
- MH (Master Hunter)

Herding Test
- HT (Herding Tested)
- PT (Pre-Trial Tested)
- HS (Herding Started)
- HI (Herding Intermediate)
- HX (Herding Excellent)

Lure Coursing
- JC (Junior Courser)
- SC (Senior Courser)
- MC (Master Courser)

Earthdog
- JE (Junior Earthdog)
- SE (Senior Earthdog)
- ME (Master Earthdog)

MADISON SQUARE GARDEN CENTER
Seventh to Eighth Aves. & 31st to 33rd Streets, New York City

22nd ANNUAL DOG SHOW
THE WESTMINSTER KENNEL CLUB
MONDAY and TUESDAY, FEBRUARY 8 and 9, 1999

EXHIBITOR

NOT VALID UNLESS SIGNED

NOTICE Always, upon leaving this show, if you wish to return the same day, present this
Ticket at Exhibitor Entrance and obtain a Return Check. This Ticket without a
Return Check or Return Check without this ticket is not good for Admission.

TUES. FEB. 9
№ 2695 2
EXHIBITOR
THE WESTMINSTER KENNEL CLUB
123rd ANNUAL DOG SHOW
MADISON SQUARE GARDEN CENTER

MON. FEB. 8
№ 2695 1
EXHIBITOR
THE WESTMINSTER KENNEL CLUB
123rd ANNUAL DOG SHOW
MADISON SQUARE GARDEN CENTER

The world's oldest dog show is the Westminster Kennel Club Dog Show, which takes place annually in New York City. The group finals are completely televised, and the show has an attendance of more than 50,000 people per day.

INDEX

My Brittany

PUT YOUR PUPPY'S FIRST PICTURE HERE

Dog's Name _____

Date _____ Photographer _____